DR JORDI ROBERT-RIBES

CONNECTING FORWARD

ADVANCED NETWORKING FOR EXECUTIVES
CHANGING JOBS, COMPANY, INDUSTRY OR COUNTRY

Copyright © 2012 Jordi Robert-Ribes

Illustrations by www.silvialanga.com

The moral right of the author has been asserted.

Apart from any fair dealing for the purposes of research or private study, or criticism or review, as permitted under the Copyright, Designs and Patents Act 1988, this publication may only be reproduced, stored or transmitted, in any form or by any means, with the prior permission in writing of the publishers, or in the case of reprographic reproduction in accordance with the terms of licences issued by the Copyright Licensing Agency. Enquiries concerning reproduction outside those terms should be sent to the publishers.

The information presented herein represents the views of the author as of the date of publication. This book is presented for informational purposes only. Due to the rate at which conditions change, the author reserves the right to alter and update his opinions at any time. While every attempt has been made to verify the information in this book, the author does not assume any responsibility for errors, inaccuracies, or omissions.

Matador
9 Priory Business Park,
Wistow Road, Kibworth Beauchamp,
Leicestershire. LE8 0RX
Tel: (+44) 116 279 2299
Fax: (+44) 116 279 2277
Email: books@troubador.co.uk
Web: www.troubador.co.uk/matador

ISBN 978 1780880 495

British Library Cataloguing in Publication Data.
A catalogue record for this book is available from the British Library.

Typeset in 11pt Bembo by Troubador Publishing Ltd, Leicester, UK
Printed and bound in the UK by TJ International, Padstow, Cornwall

Matador is an imprint of Troubador Publishing Ltd

Contents

Let's Get the Basics Right	**1**
Yes, you can help your new colleagues!	1
Book structure	2
Your attitude towards *helping others*	3
Growing your network, one node at a time	4
Weak ties are stronger	7
Your self-introduction: a memorable single sentence	9
To speak or to write?	10
The magic of 'thank you'	12
Moving through uncharted territory	13
Networking is like building new roads	14
Surveying	15
Constructing	16
Maintaining	17
Old basic skills required to use the Internet	17
Network Inside a Corporation	**19**
Surveying the corporation	20
Adapt your self-introduction	21
Say 'hello' from your contacts	22
Move around the corporation	25
Listen, listen, listen	29
Building	31
Invest time while eating lunch	32
Make yourself even more visible via larger groups	34

Be a helping hand	36
Seek 'helping brains'	39
Maintaining	42
Bring back value to your colleagues	42
Add your contacts to the corporation's network	44
Develop trust through informal shared activities	46

Network in a New Industry	**49**
Surveying your new industry	50
Speak the industry's language	50
Subscribe to trade magazines	54
Building	55
Reactivate old connections and cultivate more 'weak ties'	55
Don't be just an attendee at conferences	57
Become involved in associations	62
Write articles in trade magazines	65
Phone, meet, and phone again!	66
Prepare even harder before every meeting	71
Maintaining	72
Don't rush	73
Develop bridges with your previous industries	74

Networking Across a New Country	**77**
Surveying	78
Clarify your objective	78
Learn about current events	80
Explore the country's culture	82
Prepare to build trust step by step	87
Building	90

Visit your new country	90
Connect via your weak ties	93
Interview executives	98
Help in trade missions	100
Join the right clubs	102
Dinner at home	107
Maintaining	111
Visit back home	112
Keep reporting back	113
Practice and Adapt Your Learning	**116**
Practice the tips, one by one	116
Adapt the tips	116
Further Reading and References	**118**
Books	118
Other references	119

INTRODUCTION

Let's Get the Basics Right

Yes, you can help your new colleagues!

You might be moving into a new company, progressing into a new industry, or even relocating to a new country. You might be an experienced networker and networking is not new to you.

Now you face a new challenge; succeeding in a new territory. How are you going to create your network from scratch?

Networking is 'leveraging' your relationships for mutual gain. There is no such thing as successful one-way networking. Everyone needs to get something out of it. If you are the only one who benefits from your network, it will not be sustainable over time. If you give nothing, you will receive nothing. If you bring value to your relationships – for instance by sending useful articles your network contacts will reciprocate and bring value back to you. We are all human. We like to receive as well as give.

However, now you are in unknown territory. You can see clearly how your new colleagues can help you. How on earth can you help them? You might feel there is not much you can do for them. They know the territory much better than you do. They do not need your help. They might even have their own turf and feel threatened by your arrival. If these are some of your fears, relax, take a deep breath, and keep reading. You can be successful in your new territory. Networking will be crucial to that success.

Book structure

This book has an introduction and three parts. The introduction will review some basic networking techniques. I will also introduce the analogy of networking and road building.

The following three parts discuss each situation in which you might want to improve your networking techniques after going into new territory.

The first part (*Network Inside a Corporation*) will guide your efforts when you change position within your company or move to another corporation.

The second part (*Network in a New Industry*) deals with networking when you change sectors.

The third part (*Networking Across a New Country*) considers networking when you change countries.

Throughout the book you will read real cases (case studies) of people who have used networking in some of their career changes. I interviewed these people during the information gathering stage for this book. They are very diverse, from vice-presidents of public corporations to freelance professionals. You can, most probably, identify with one of them

Your attitude towards helping others

Networking needs a genuinely helpful attitude and lots of practice.

Like most things in life, effective networking cannot be achieved by just following the steps in a recipe book. It is a skill that comes with practice. Probably you learned rudimentary networking during your previous career and now you need to upgrade it to suit your new situation. You will need to change or improve some of your networking techniques. This book will help you do that. However, the key to success will remain the same: your attitude towards *helping others*. If you only want to *receive*, it will be very hard for people to help you.

If you do not greet, they will not greet you. If you do not help, they will not help you. If you do not give information, they will not give you information. It's the 'boomerang effect'.

Networking needs practice. Advanced networking needs a *lot* of practice! You didn't learn to ride a bike by reading how to do it. You went to the park and practiced. When you first learned networking, you learned by doing. Now you need to go to the next level: advanced networking. Reading a book, this one or any other, is not enough. You need to get out and apply your *reading* so that it becomes *learning*. Let's go back to our bike analogy. You can ride a bike and hope to do the Amateur Tour de France. You need to read a book on how to train for it. However, the most important part will be getting out and training!

Back in 1980, Patricia Wagner and Leif Smith wrote, 'Networks are processes, not institutions.' Rail networks are fixed networks. Our personal networks are living networks. They live thanks to our attitude towards them. The tools we use are just that: tools. They need power so that they can move. That power is your attitude towards helping others. The same type of power (your attitude) is needed whether you are within your comfort zone (with your friends or colleagues) or you are moving into uncharted territory.

Somehow the petrol is more important than the pipes. How you relate to your network is more important than the network itself. Lyz Linch puts it very clearly when she writes in her book *Smart Networking*, 'To me the secret lies less in who's in your network and more in how you relate to your network.'

Note the difference between the following two people. One communicates with his network only when sending Christmas cards. The other one interacts every couple of months with the people in her network. It is obvious that the former is someone with an address book while the latter has a network!

Along the same lines, Herminia Ibarra and Mark Hunter, professors at INSEAD, remind us, 'A network lives and thrives only when it is used.' You must keep your network alive even during periods when you feel you don't need it. You will probably need it sooner than you expect. If you let your network cool down too much, you might not be able to revive it! There are many examples of leading executives whose careers stalled as soon as they entered uncharted territory. Some of them had stopped networking while in their previous roles. They had only retained a few acquaintances in their network. There were people in their network but they didn't relate to them. They had a passive attitude towards networking.

Growing your network, one node at a time

You meet new people via other contacts. Thank them.

First things first. How do you grow a network? Answer: by adding relevant **nodes**.

LET'S GET THE BASICS RIGHT / 5

What steps should you follow to grow your network? Let me remind you that, in networking, there is no such thing as right or wrong. The following steps offer you a possible route to follow.

We grow our network via other people. We need to thank them.

Let's concentrate on the 'adding' part and in particular on the occasions when someone (the **adviser**) recommends that you (the **networker**) contact someone else (the **referral**) because that person can provide you with relevant information. The steps below could be the standard ones.

1. The adviser recommends that you contact the referral.

2. You arrange a meeting with the referral where you:

>2a. Give the referral valuable information (that is, information from you, the networker, to the referral).

>2b. Gather information relevant to you (the networker).

3. You ask for further recommendations and referrals. (If this happens, the referral becomes an adviser, so the wheel keeps turning again to step 2).

4. You subsequently thank the referral. You can do this by email, post or other 'non-synchronous'[1] methods (e.g. not by phone). This serves to remind the referral about you and your needs.

5. You thank the adviser for the contact. The possible methods are the same as for the previous point.

Some steps are easy to forget because of work pressures and deadlines. This can happen not only to the novice networker but also to the experienced one. The steps most often forgotten are: giving valuable information (2a) and thanking people (4-5).

Relationships with people very different from you can be most valuable.

---

[1] A 'non-synchronous' method is one in which there is no need to communicate at the same time, people may not be connected exactly the same time, for example, mail and e-mail.

Weak ties are stronger

The more diverse your network, the more valuable it will be.

Some people have a very large network of contacts with persons very similar to themselves. Other people have a smaller network of very diverse individuals. Which of these two types of network do you think is more valuable? The diverse one, of course!

In 1973, when he was at Johns Hopkins University, Mark Granovetter published a seminal article about the 'strength of weak ties'. He wrote, 'Whatever is to be diffused can reach a larger number of people … when passed through weak ties rather than strong.'

In a nutshell, the argument is as follows. You tend to meet people who are similar to yourself. They also know people similar to themselves and, of course, similar to you. This creates an **inbred network** that lacks diversity. All in all, it makes for a rather ineffective network when you are trying to locate new information or reach new people.

Your network will reach further via the weak ties. These weak ties are the ones formed by people with whom you spend little time, have no emotional links, and with whom you share no confidences.

Granovetter defines the strength of a tie as 'a combination of the amount of time, the emotional intensity, the intimacy (mutual confiding), and the reciprocal services which characterize the tie.' Thus it is easy to imagine why strong ties are more likely to 'just happen' without much effort on your part. However, weak ties are a different animal. By definition, you will need to be *active* to acquire new weak ties.

Professor Gargiulo (from INSEAD) goes even further. He warns that homogenous networks can be a liability. If only people similar to yourself compose your network, it can turn into a set of blinkers. Such a network can be very comforting but will soon become a liability. However, if you have a sparse network (with lots of weak-ties), it can help you to reach well beyond your own corporation. Even so, do not be fooled into thinking that by having lots of weak ties, you have a huge network. According to Gargiulo, your core network will have hardly more than thirty people. The weak ties are useful because they do not need major maintenance, and they can be reactivated when necessary.

Research from the University of Virginia and Accenture shows that 'Top performers tend to invest in relationships that extend their expertise and help them avoid learning biases and career traps.'

It is via weak ties that you will reach people in unrelated networks. For instance, when I needed information about high-street real estate I had to activate as many weak ties as possible. My strong ties were mainly in the telecommunications-engineering sector. They could not take me far in my information gathering endeavours.

Using my strong ties I could easily reach academics and even deans of universities. However, I had to invest in nurturing weak ties so that I could reach out to the relevant people in the retail sector. Notice that I use the words 'invest' and 'nurture'. Both actions are extremely important with weak ties. You need to keep in mind that gathering information via weak ties is much slower than via strong ties.

Weak ties can take you to places that strong ties could never dream of.

Your self-introduction: a memorable single sentence

People will remember you thanks to your self-introduction.

A self-introduction is a memorable single sentence that you can say to people when meeting for the first time. It needs to be memorable, particularly when you are at a large gathering. This will help people to remember you among the many other individuals whom they will meet that day. Keith Ferrazzi, in *Never Eat Alone*, calls it the Personal Branding Message that succinctly describes your unique value proposition. For Ivan Misner, your Unique Selling Proposition should be tailored down to twelve words, which is the average human attention span.

'Hello, my name is Jordi. I nurture companies to help them blossom. I work as investments director at ABC Ltd.' This would be my self-introduction when attending investment or entrepreneurial events.

For instance, 'Hello, my name is John. I am a doctor' would be harder to remember than 'Hello, my name is John. I help people see the wonderful world around them. I'm an eye doctor.'

The self-introduction is not your 'elevator pitch', which would be longer. Neither is it your CV spoken at a fast pace! The self-introduction serves to establish rapport with the other person. It will allow the other people to have an initial idea of how you could help them. Most networking books offer advice on how to craft your self-introduction[2].

---

2 In 'How to Work a Room' see pages 21-23 and 83-84. In 'Smart Networking' go to pages 45-62. In 'The Networking Survival Guide' refer to pages 124-125. In 'Let's Connect' turn to pages 110-112. In 'El éxito en seis cafés' (in Spanish) look at pages 236-239. In 'Booster sa carrière grâce au Réseau' (in French), check 'cocktail-pitch' on page 39.

You should adapt your self-introduction to each situation. Thus your introductory sentence will be different if you were at a business conference rather than at your children's Speech Day. If networking is not second nature to you, it is important that you practice the delivery of your self-introduction. Once you are confident with it, you can easily adapt the contents to each situation.

Your self-introduction is an easy item to practice in safe environments. These can be within training sessions or within settings you create yourself. Here are some examples of non-business settings where you can practice your self-introduction. They are situations in which you will not feel threatened as they involve people you will probably never see again:

- When queuing (buying a ticket, boarding a plane, or any other queue you find yourself in).
- Most situations when you are holidaying in a foreign country.
- Sitting on a train that is not your usual commuter line.
- Sitting on an aeroplane.

These are just examples. You will find plenty of other situations you can use for practicing.

To speak or to write?

Don't forget the benefits of speaking over the phone.

The email is a great working tool. The phone is a great networking tool. When contacting someone for the first time, the phone is often more useful. And especially if that phone call is intended to get a face-to-face meeting. It is harder to say 'no' over the phone than via email.

This is particularly true when you are building a network in a new area or industry and you are still unknown. Sending an email with compelling information to your counterpart might prove useful. However, it's more likely that you will receive neither reply nor feedback.

One of the advantages of getting the other person on the phone is that even if you do not end up with the face-to-face meeting that you wanted, at least you may get feedback on how the industry is doing, or some other relevant information.

As David Rayback writes in *ConnectAbility*, 'One reason some of us occasionally find it difficult to communicate over the Internet is that we rely so heavily on facial and body expressions as well as eye contact that we feel somewhat lost when communicating by e-mail, especially when there's a need for nonverbal cues in the communication.' When you contact someone for the very first time the nonverbal clues are very important indeed.

This does not mean that contacting someone via email is useless or that it cannot provide an outcome. I have done it and it can work. However, the point I am trying to make here is that you should carefully choose the channel by which you contact someone for the first time.

In some cases, even most cases, the phone call allows the other person to ask you, 'Please email me with that information.' When you send the email, it is no longer a 'cold' email. It is an email that refers to the initial phone call and thus gets more attention from the recipient.

Next time you contact someone for the first time, spend a couple of minutes weighing the pros and cons of the different channels you can use. And don't give excessive weight to emails. That would be too easy!

When trying to reach someone by phone, you can be persistent. Be careful not to cross the line to being annoying. It's a very fine line. Always be polite in the voice messages you leave and when talking with the personal assistant. It will be useful to remember the personal assistant's name, and use it when phoning.

The best time of the day to phone is early morning. On the other hand, late afternoon can prove useful to reach people when their personal assistants have left. However, you will be speaking to someone who will most probably be tired and not willing to engage in friendly conversations.

When the executive answers the phone, you will briefly state your name and common relationship and then say something along the lines of 'Is this a good time for you?' or 'Do you have a couple of minutes now?' If the answer is 'No', then you ask when would be a convenient time. Make a reminder in your diary to phone back at that time or day.

The magic of 'thank you'

Always thank people who helped you along the way.

Thanking people for things they have done for you is more than a polite thing to do. It is a great networking tool.

People remember best the ones who thank them for their efforts. Sounds reasonable, doesn't it? However, it is extremely easy to forget to thank the person who introduced you to someone else, or the person who sent you useful information.

Let's suppose you activate your network in order to employ a new member in your organisation. When you achieve your objective (employing the right person), you should thank everyone you have contacted along the way. It doesn't matter if they were instrumental in the success or not. What matters is that they did put some time and effort in trying to help you. To thank them is more than a matter of appreciation. It is, as Keith Ferrazzi puts it in *Never Eat Alone*, 'An opportunity to reinforce a perception of continuity in a relationship and create an aura of goodwill.'

You can thank someone by sending a thank you note. The other person will appreciate it. In addition to the note you can add an interesting article or other token item. Then the other person will also benefit. When thanking someone, think broad. Do not narrow your thoughts into the standard thank-you note or email.

Be specific on the reason to thank him or her. Jan Vermeiren in *Let's Connect* suggests that by doing so you will 'have the highest impact and nurture the relationship'.

Moving through uncharted territory

When you are in unknown territory, networking is essential for survival.

When you are within the boundaries of your known territory, networking is useful. When you are in your city, you know where to go when you need something. When you have been working for a while in a corporation, you know whom to turn to. Networking can help you access those people, but you already know who they are.

When you move into unknown territory, networking becomes essential for survival. You do not have a map. You are moving into uncharted waters. You need your network to shed some light on your path.

Your network will not just help you to contact people. It will also help you to know *whom* to contact.

You might have just moved into a new corporation. Probably the hierarchy, the rules and the culture are completely different to those you were used to in your previous corporation. There may be no written rules here. Your network will be your lifeline.

Or you may have moved into a new industry. The players in that industry could have many different expectations of you, which may be very different from your own expectations. Even the language is different. 'Early stage' in this new industry means what in your previous industry was called 'late stage'. Your network will be your chaperon.

You may even have been parachuted into a new country. The working culture looks superficially similar to your own. However, as soon as you look into it more deeply, it is completely different. For starters the dress code may have changed, even though you believed that in your industry it was universal. The meeting protocol might be totally different. Let your network be your guide.

Networking is like building new roads

Roads need tarmac. Your network needs trust.

In my seminars and keynotes, I have found the road construction analogy very useful in illustrating the point. Building your network in uncharted territory is similar to building new roads. Roads connect towns and cities. We use them to go from one point to another. Often, they are not straight lines; instead to go from point A to point B they need to go via point C. Your network connects people. Building roads is connecting different places. Creating your network is establishing relationships between people. Roads need tarmac. Your network needs trust.

Building roads, as well as networking, involves three recurrent actions:

a) Surveying,
b) Building,
c) Maintaining.

Surveying

You want to find the relevant people for your network. It needs to be an active exercise. If you take the passive route, you could end up with a small network that is out of line with your own objectives.

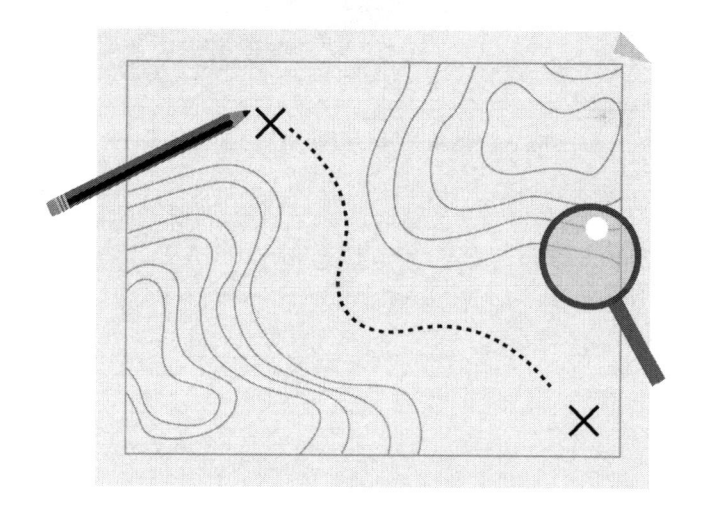

You survey the terrain.

In our road analogy, you need to continuously examine the landscape and its topography. There need to be enough new roads to cope with the traffic despite its increases or changes. Assume that you will lose some roads, which cannot be restored. You need to know where to build new routes. Otherwise, over time, your network might disappear!

Constructing

You build roads on the surveyed land.

You want some of the people you have met to become part of your network. You want to convert contacts into links. In order to achieve this, you need to take steps to attract them to your network.

In our road analogy, the tarmac will settle well in some parts of the road. Where it doesn't settle, the surface will be unusable. This will depend on incidents outside your control (terrain, climate, etc). However, you still need to build the road and do whatever you can to make it operational.

Maintaining

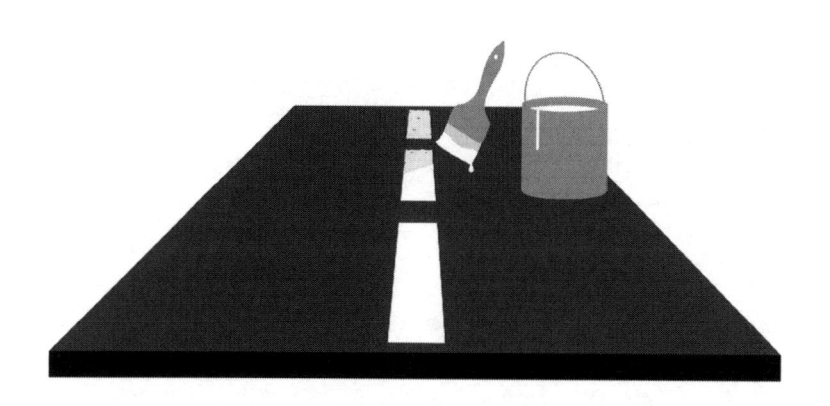

You maintain your roads.

You must provide value to your links so that they stay in your network. The value you give often comes in the form of information that helps them solve their current problems. However, it can also come in many other forms, as we will see throughout this book.

In our road analogy, you need to maintain the roads that you build. You cannot expect that they will remain intact forever. You need to use the roads so that they do not get covered in rocks and grass. Regularly using your network makes it stronger.

Old basic skills required to use the Internet

Social networking websites are new tools for networking. But don't be fooled into thinking that such tools will be all you need to network. This is one of the biggest mistakes some managers make. They create an account in a business networking site (for instance,

LinkedIn) and believe they have an instant network in their new territory.

Online tools cannot be a substitute for face-to-face meetings or even a personalised letter. The impression that a potential contact will have of you will be completely different if you send a personalised letter with a nice stamp than if you send the standard introduction automatically created by LinkedIn. Of course they will prefer the former!

Online tools cannot think on your behalf. They will not give you ideas on how you can be of benefit to your contacts. They will not write personalised letters. They will not make phone calls. They will not meet people face-to-face and build trust into a relationship. You will have to do all these things yourself. Online tools will be a medium, not an end in themselves.

The tips in this book will point you in the right direction for the use of online tools. In some cases online tools are very useful, in others they are of no use at all or can even be a trap to avoid.

PART 1

Network Inside a Corporation

Congratulations on your new position! If you have changed position within the same corporation or you have moved into a new one, this part of the book is for you.

Even if your job starts in a few weeks time, you must start building (or reinforcing) your network. You want a soft landing in your new job, and having contacts inside the corporation will help you achieve it.

Some big corporations are very much aware of the importance of a network for new recruits. For example, PricewaterhouseCoopers offers a five-month program called Genesis Park for young leaders focused on building networks across the company. Participants are very diverse. This fosters relationships created during the five months between people from diverse departments.

Throughout this chapter, I will use the word 'corporation' instead of 'company'. The main reason is because we tend to perceive corporations as bigger than companies. The bigger the organisation, the more critical will be your networking efforts. If you join a twenty-person company, your internal networking efforts will be quite straightforward and mainly personal relationship skills. However, if that small company is in a different sector from your previous one, you will get value reading part *Network in a New Industry*.

H. Bommelaer in his book *Booster sa carrière grâce au Réseau* (*Boost Your Career Thanks to Your Network*) suggests that good networking during your first days in the corporation will help you get through the initial trial period and avoid being in the five percent of managers who fail.

If you want to further advance your career in your new corporation, networking will stack the odds on your side. Professor Ronald Burt from the Chicago Booth School of Business shows why good networking helps managers advance their careers faster: 'People who have contacts in separate groups have a competitive advantage because we live in a system of bureaucracies, and bureaucracies create walls.' Furthermore, research published in the *MIT Sloan Management Review* by Professor Rob Cross proves that 'what really distinguishes high performers from the rest of the pack is their ability to maintain and leverage personal networks.'

Surveying the corporation

Listen. Greet. Introduce yourself. Move around.

Adapt your self-introduction

Prepare and rehearse a self-introduction that answers the main questions that your colleagues will have about you (such as 'can you help me?' or 'are you a threat to me?').

You probably have a well-rehearsed self-introduction. Let me remind you that it is a memorable sentence that you say when you meet people for the first time (see the chapter *Your self-introduction: a memorable single sentence*). Now you need to adapt it to your intra-corporation networking. This self-introduction, even if brief, needs to answer the following questions:

- What is your role in the corporation?
- What do you bring to your position?
- Why are you not a threat to your peers?

For example, you could say, 'My name is Steve. I've just joined XYZ Corp within the New Media department to execute an internet customer acquisition plan. My previous roles were with Yahoo Europe and Google Australasia as media technology director. The skills of the printed magazine editors here, at XYZ Corp, are impressive. I look forward to collaborating with you all and learning about the best practices you have.'

You must prepare your self-introduction *before* you start your job. During the interview process you will gather information about the corporation and how you will fit in. You can read the recent annual reports and press clippings to prepare for your new job. Such information will allow you to have a self-introduction that is succinct but full of information.

Let me stress the importance of having an initial version of your self-introduction before your very first day at the corporation. You do not want to replicate what happened to me. The fourth day in my new job I caught the lift on the ground floor and was alone in it. On the first floor, one person entered the lift: the CEO! I knew his office was on level 31. I should have been able to produce a self-introduction during the thirty-floor run. However, as the floors were going by, I felt more and more naked.

When we reached the 28th floor I started mumbling 'Hello, I just...'

But then he said in a very straightforward way, 'Bye, have a great day.'

We had reached the 31st floor. Game over! During the many years I worked at that corporation I never ever again had the opportunity to meet the CEO. I missed my only chance to leave a great impression.

Of course, you need to continuously adapt the self-introduction so that it remains valid. You will adjust it as you learn more about the culture of the corporation and its departments. You will also take into account how different colleagues react to it. You do not want to have a self-introduction that generates too much surprise. You want to dispel any myths or fears generated by the corporation offering you that position.

Remember the adage: 'Spectacular achievement is always preceded by spectacular preparation.'

Say 'hello' from your contacts

When you notify people in your network about the new job, some might know key people in your new corporation. Meet them!

After accepting the job, you thanked the many people who had helped you get that job. You thanked the people who paved your path during your job search. Some of these people suggested that you give their regards to someone they know in that corporation. You might even have prompted them to do so by saying something along the lines of 'Would you like me to see someone on your behalf in that corporation?'

From the very first day of your job, you will contact several people on behalf of your contacts. You will do it preferably by phone or in person. You would only use email if it were absolutely the only medium available. (See the chapter *To speak or to write?* for further comments on the advantage of phone or in person.) As William Byham recommends in an article in the *Harvard Business Review*, 'It's imperative to start forging deliberate connections within the first thirty to sixty days after [starting a new role]'. The recommendations you get will help you in those initial efforts. In our road network analogy, your contacts have done some surveying for you!

The best days to contact those people are at the beginning of the week, and the best time is early in the day. Executives are often more relaxed in the morning. The meetings should be very brief and to the point. You do not want to be seen as someone who spends most of the time socialising at work. If during the discussion you feel you should have a deeper conversation with that person, schedule time for a proper meeting with clear goals.

You should keep a clear focus on your objectives for those brief conversations:

- Gather information on how you can help that particular person, his/her team, or the whole corporation.
- Understand the corporate culture.

- Ask him/her for the names of other people within the corporation whom you should talk to.
- Make yourself visible within the corporation.

While you contact those executives, you will benefit from getting to know other important staff: their personal assistants. They are the gatekeepers and you want to have them on your side. Remember their names and say thank you to them after you have spoken to the executive.

Of course, you will send a quick note or make a brief phone call to thank the people who recommended that you meet those people (see chapter *The magic of 'thank you'*). They will be delighted to hear news about the people they know, and they might recommend you contact even more people within the corporation. In that case, do contact those people promptly. This will give you a reputation for professionalism and efficiency.

There are many reasons that might make you forget to thank the advisers, such as being drowned in your new job. One way to ensure that you do not skip it is to put it in your diary. For instance, you can schedule in your diary a thirty-minute period every Friday to thank the people who have helped you along the way.

On the other hand, during the hiring process, several people interviewed you. They can also be excellent starting points for your network. You should pay particular attention to including them in your initial networking efforts during your very first days at the corporation. Of course, thanking them for the successful interview is the bare minimum.

Move around the corporation

Go to other departments to bump into new people. You will start building valuable bridges across the corporation that will help your career advancement.

Armed with a big smile and your self-introduction (see chapter *Adapt your self-introduction*) you should explore the corporation by moving around it.

Your first weeks are a great opportunity to venture into areas of the building or the offices where you might not go again in the future. For example, let's say you are in the marketing department, which is located on the 23rd floor of a big office building. You can go into the lift and step out at any floor. It might be the floor reserved for the CEO and top executives, which might be locked to other staff. In that case, just get into the lift and start again. Otherwise, walk around the floor and notice what is there.

You have a big smile in your face and say hello to the people you cross on your way. You will notice that some of them will just say hello and move on. However, someone will be open to having a short chat. In that case, your first weapon has worked: your smile. Now you should use your second weapon: your self-introduction. You state that you started your job recently, and then introduce yourself. The other person might do likewise. If he/she doesn't, you can easily ask something along the lines of 'I came to this department to get to know the corporation better. So what is your role in this department?' This can lead to a brief conversation about their department and its relationship with yours. You might uncover some opportunities for collaboration between the departments or some ways in which your previous expertise can help that person or his/her department.

Don't be afraid of going one step further and asking for advice on who else in that department might be worth talking to. Remember that you are 'surveying' that corporation and the more views you can gather, the better. You will be surprised how often colleagues want to introduce you to other colleagues.

Be careful not to be perceived as a 'wanderer'. You are not casually walking around the corporation or killing time. You have a very specific and work-related objective (better understanding of the corporation). The following are things you can do to avoid being perceived as a wanderer:

- Do not have your discussions at the coffee shop, water-cooler or kitchenette.
- Carry a small notepad to take notes about the things you learn about other departments.[3]
- Keep your discussions brief, up to a maximum of five minutes. If some topic pops up that would warrant a more in-depth discussion, you should schedule a meeting (even if an informal one) with that person.

Academic research shows repeatedly the importance of having connections that span the organisation. For instance, a joint study by the University of Virginia and Accenture shows that 'Top performers tend to occupy network positions that bridge otherwise disconnected clusters of people.' It even proves that 'people who bridge subgroups are much more likely to be in the top twenty percent (as determined by performance reviews).'

---

[3] Even if you would prefer typing your notes on your smart-phone for easy future retrieval, a notepad has one big advantage. When you write on a notepad it is very clear to everyone that you are writing notes about your conversation. If you type into your smart phone, the other person might wonder whether you are taking notes or just texting your spouse!

Moving around the corporation will help you add valuable nodes to your network. As you know, it is not the *quantity* of the nodes that is important but their *quality*. The figure shows the importance of linking into different parts of the corporation.

Joe and Sam have the same number of connections (five). Let's imagine that both started at the corporation on the very same day. While Sam focused on creating his network *inside* his own department, Joe was meeting people from *across the organisation*. Most probably Joe is now in a position to exploit his links to different departments.

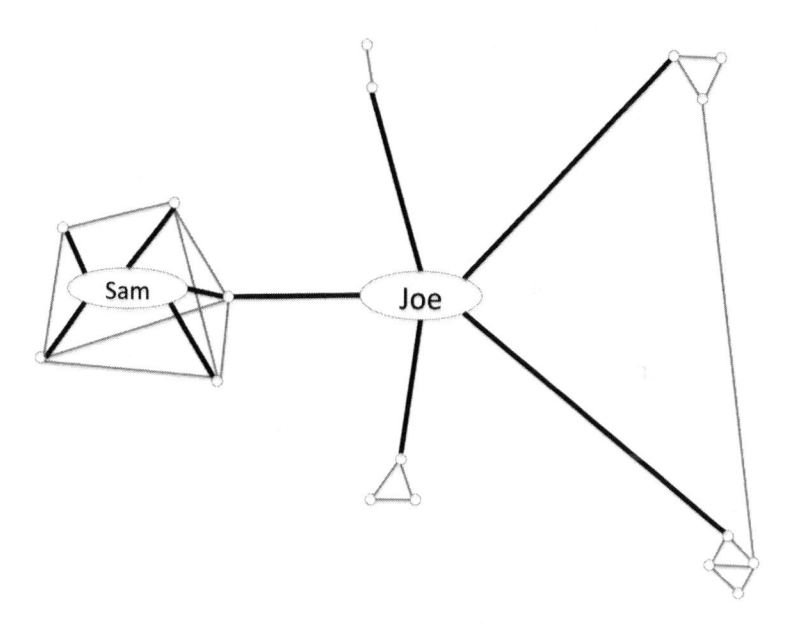

The importance of valuable nodes.
Joe's five links are more valuable than Sam's.

Research from INSEAD reinforces the point. Its organizational behaviour professor, Martin Gargiulo, proves that managers who bridge between separate groups can 'monitor information more effectively than it can be monitored bureaucratically. They move information faster, and to more people, than memos.'

> ### Case Study: J Patrick (JP) Bewley
>
> (Vice President, Global Consulting and Agency Services, Acxiom Corporation)
>
> In 2008 JP joined Acxiom, a listed corporation. He was hired to initiate a new global marketing strategy practice within the corporation.
>
> Acxiom is a broad and diverse corporation. During the first six months he focused on 'doing favours and helping people'. He travelled extensively to meet colleagues in different parts of the organisation. He realised that anything he could do that was related to clients or deals would be instrumental in building his colleagues' trust. He helped them with rehearsals and dry runs for presentations. He also volunteered to give talks in front of customers at sales presentations.
>
> At the beginning he cast his net wide then later narrowed it to focus on key individuals. He was always open-minded about whom to meet, while keeping in mind that new people are often recruited into the business. He liked diversity in the people who surround him. He often remembered his former boss and mentor's advice: 'When two people always agree, you don't need one of them.'
>
> Before meeting a colleague he prepared extensively. He read many reports on the subject matter from technology and market research companies (e.g. Forrester Research). He then synthesised the main messages and included his own points of view. If meeting face-to-face was not possible, he used video-conferencing. He felt it was a good tool to help in building trust.

> When he changed half his team, he ensured they moved around the corporation in order to gain visibility with the rest of the company. They were briefed not just to 'move around', but to help colleagues achieve their goals.
>
> When JP's boss resigned, some of the people from JP's network advocated that he be considered for the vacant position. He was offered the job and accepted gratefully. He now has responsibility for about 8% of the corporation's employees and 10% of the corporate P&L.
>
> The relationship building efforts he made during his first six months were instrumental in his career progress within the corporation.
>
> His advice:
>
> - Do a lot of favours to a lot of people. Do as much as you can to help them achieve their goals.
> - Don't aim at large wins immediately. Plan for small, quick victories.

Listen, listen, listen

Keep your ears wide open during the first weeks.
You will learn about things that you will never hear again.

There are lots of things that are not written in the induction materials that you receive when joining a corporation (if you receive any at all!). The way to uncover such things is to listen between the lines. This is what Liz Lynch calls the 'fine art of listening' in her book *Smart Networking*. She even has good news for the shy ones among us: 'While the introverts may hold back from the crowd a bit, we tend to be good listeners.'

When you talk to people, both inside and outside the corporation, you can gather excellent information if you use your brain at its full potential. Your brain can understand 600 words per minute. However, your body can only produce 140 words per minute. Thus you have plenty of spare capacity when listening to someone. Use it to understand the underlying issues of what is said as well as to ask the right questions. If your mind drifts towards other issues, focus explicitly on the person who is talking to you. Asking confirmation questions will help you keep your focus and will verify that you have understood correctly. An example of a confirmation question is: 'If I understand correctly, you feel that this department should be split into two departments.'

Listening between the lines becomes very important during your first days within the corporation. Often you will be approached by different staff who will try to get you on their side of an internal conflict. Since you are unaware of the conflict, you might take a side even without knowing it. If you had listened between the lines you might have seen what that person was trying to do. Be particularly cautious with colleagues who show unfounded interest in talking often to you.

You should take advantage of not being trapped in established network rigidity, as some of your colleagues might be. After a few weeks at the corporation, some staff will not be as open with you and thus you will uncover less information by listening to them. They may be more taciturn because they might perceive, even if it's just their imagination, that you have already taken sides (with or against them, it doesn't really matter). Since they are no longer trying to persuade you to take their side, what they say may have less value to you when you are listening between the lines.

While extroverts tend to be better talkers, introverts tend to be better listeners. They tend to be able to uncover more information from the same spoken segment. This does not mean that if you are an extrovert you cannot listen between the lines. Not at all! It means that you might need to increase your efforts to actively listen.

There are many things you can do to listen more effectively. Jan Vermeiren, author of *Let's Connect*, provides several examples:

- Give your full attention to the conversation.
- Listen with the intention to gather information.
- Have the other person talk more than yourself.

Keep your ears open during the whole of your career. Do not stop listening after a few months in your new job. A joint study by the University of Virginia and Accenture clearly advises, 'High networkers often create their own luck by being more attuned to the network around them.'

Building

Use lunchtime. Participate in groups. Offer help. Ask for help.

Invest time while eating lunch

Enjoy lunch with colleagues while you load trust into your network.

With so many new things to learn and do during the first weeks, you might be tempted to avoid 'wasting' time eating lunch. Thus, you might just grab a sandwich and eat at your desk. Don't do it! Instead you should *invest* time while eating lunch.

You want to use your time getting to know new people within the corporation and building trust with the people you already know. Keith Ferrazzi wrote a best seller on this very same topic: *Never Eat Alone*.

There are lots of things you can do instead of eating a three-course lunch in a fancy restaurant or having a long lunch chatting with your friends at the local pub.

For instance, you can go with a colleague to buy a sandwich and eat it together in the park next to your building. This will allow you to build trust with the colleague by discussing different topics. It does not need to be an entirely project related conversation. You can ask about previous projects or assignments. You can gather information about the corporation politics or turf battles. You can even clarify your previous roles and how you plan to use your skills in your current job. Of course, you might talk every now and then about completely non-work related matters such as sports, holiday destinations, or even children's schools. However, since you are a focused professional, you want to keep your discussions within a work related framework. You might not want to befriend every new colleague. So keep the in-depth non-work-related discussions for the colleagues whom you will invite for dinner at your place or whom you will see outside work.

You can also ask people where they recommend having lunch. You can try the following: Around lunchtime you go into a common area or take the lift. You will see employees who seem to be going out for lunch. Some of them are alone. Ask them for recommendations on where to have lunch. You might have unpleasant surprises, like the answer I once got: 'Go and see for yourself. There are lots of places around to have lunch. You don't expect me to recommend a place, do you?' Such an answer tells a lot about that person! However, about half the time you will get a straight recommendation. Other times, you will even be invited to join them so that you can 'discover' their favourite place. This becomes a great occasion to get to know new people. Remember that they can become an excellent weak tie in your network (see chapter *Weak ties are stronger*).

Why not join a weekly lunch get-together? Often, groups of employees have a day of the week when they meet for lunch. If you have identified such a group and know one of them, you should ask to join them. Do not be intrusive. The first time you should just go with the flow and discuss the topics that are on the table. Of course, you will need to introduce yourself to the members of the group that you don't yet know. You will use your fine-tuned self-introduction (see chapter *Adapt your self-introduction*). This is as far as you should go about yourself on your first lunch. Add value to the conversation instead of hijacking it.

You can start a regular weekly lunch get-together. If you haven't identified any group that meets for lunch, why don't you start a new group? There are several things to keep in mind. The group should be small enough so that everyone can interact with everyone else. Ensure that you have variety in the group. Try to get people from different parts of the corporation so that you generate trust with other departments. You might even want to start several groups. One could be departmental, while the other could be inter-departmental.

Make yourself even more visible via larger groups

Gain visibility by putting yourself in front of internal groups, such as at weekly meetings, special interest groups or even by creating your own event.

As previously discussed, you can gain visibility with one-on-one meetings (see chapters *Adapt your self-introduction* and *Move around the corporation*). Moreover, you can also make yourself visible with larger groups. The well-known Hollywood maxim 'Invisibility is a fate far worse than failure' also applies in most corporations.

The following are some of the opportunities to put yourself in front of a group of colleagues.

Weekly meetings

Most departments, groups or divisions have regular meetings (monthly or weekly). Make an explicit effort to attend them. In fact you need to do more than just attend them, you need to participate in them, not just go there and listen. When someone asks for opinions, put yours forward. When a project needs volunteers, make yourself available. If people give updates on current projects, prepare what you are going to say instead of improvising on the fly.

Bring a cake! Some environments are more prone to such opportunities. In any change of corporation in my career, I have tried bringing a cake or cookies to my first weekly meeting. It is a good way to 'sweeten' your way into that department. Remember to bring some paper towels; if the table ends up a complete mess, this is what might stay in your colleagues' minds.

If you are not inclined to bring food items, bring whatever suits your nature. You could bring some famous quotes and read them aloud. A funnier idea would be to bring lottery tickets and give them away. A more decorative one would be to take a bouquet of flowers and place it in the centre of the table.

Whatever you do at your first weekly meeting should fit your personality. Do not force yourself into doing something you would not like to do; your colleagues might perceive it as artificial.

Special Interest Groups

Some corporations put together special interest groups (SIG). Staff from different departments who share some interest form a SIG. These people would not meet during regular projects. They benefit from the SIG meetings and the corporation gains from the common knowledge created. For instance, your corporation could have the Cross Cultural Issues SIG. Managers who have been on international assignments (or might be on one shortly) could form this SIG.

If your corporation has SIGs in place, observe which SIG you could add more value to, and join it. Once again, the important factor is the value you can add to the group. You may naturally gravitate towards the group that would give you more benefit or the one where you would have more fun. Change the 'you' into 'them' and choose the group where *they* can get more benefit from *you*.

Create your own event

You might even create an event. Let me provide a personal example of what I mean.

After joining a big telecommunications corporation, I created a monthly event to discuss new technologies that would hit the market in about two years time. Each month we had an external expert present a specific new technology. It was a short-and-sweet event before the regular working day started. It was short because it lasted thirty minutes. It was sweet because a light breakfast was provided. The event was open to all staff. However, we explicitly sent invitations to the departments that would benefit the most from the technology being presented that month.

Those events were not convenient for me. The main problem was that organizing an event early in the day was hard as our children were very young at the time. However, that was the most convenient time for the staff who would benefit from the event. The usual networking exercise of putting 'them' first guided my choice.

Be a helping hand

Be on the lookout for ways to help your colleagues, both in your department and across the corporation.

After your first month in the corporation you should know many people there. You have met some of them during your regular job. You have met others through your surveying activities (see the chapters on *Surveying the corporation*). You might come across some of them during your day. Be on the lookout for ways you can help them, even if only a little. This will build up the value of your link with them. Some of those will even become very useful weak ties in your network (see chapter *Weak ties are stronger*).

Your help can be straightforward such as by carrying something heavy for someone. However, you should look for more value added actions.

For example, Helen expresses some difficulty in reaching someone in your department: 'John is so busy these days that it's very hard getting five minutes with him.' John might be located near your desk. You can help Helen identify which times of the day John seems more approachable. You might even go one step further. Back at your desk, you can tell John that Helen is trying to reach him.

You might even realise that you have some information (a book, an article, or a piece of software) that can be of very good use to the person you are talking to. Offer to find it and send it over.

There are two things you should be aware of when volunteering information. You need to be non-threatening. The other person needs to perceive your real motive: giving the information for his benefit, not because you're implying that he doesn't have the information to do his job properly. Do *not* say that someone else (another company or another country) uses that information effectively. Do not say, 'When I worked in Japan we did this and shortened the delivery time by two weeks'. Say instead something like, 'If we did this, we might be able to shorten the delivery time by two weeks, the way some other companies have done. What do you think?' The information conveyed is practically the same in both sentences. However, the latter will be more 'digestible' while the former might generate some 'avoid-as-not-built-here' reactions.

When a colleague organises an event, more often than not, the biggest risk is too few people turning up at the event. Volunteer to distribute and forward information about the event. The organiser will appreciate your help. You can distribute information via email. However, talking to other people about the event often proves more useful. Thanks to your initial networking efforts, you know people in many departments. You might be the only way they get to know about the event. This will let you start capitalising on the connections you have created with distant departments within the corporation. The further away the other department is, the more valuable your connection will be.

> ### Case Study: Amy Jenner
>
> (Vice President Sales, Pfizer)
>
> Amy has experienced several mergers during her career.
>
> During the first merger, she thought, 'Well, a merger is a merger', so she didn't check who was on the other side or how they got things done. As time went by, Amy had to learn the hard way that trust is not transferred. Once within the new organisation you have to build your credibility and trustworthiness all over again.
>
> When another merger appeared on the horizon, Amy knew what to do.
>
> This time she set herself clear goals. She prioritised building a network over building functional expertise. The latter comes almost automatically when the former is in place. 'Networking is understanding how the work is done.'
>
> Amy looked at the functional areas of the organisation with which they were merging. She assessed the platform and systems that they had in operation. Amy made a list of people with whom she needed to build a trusting relationship. She even drew a map to identify how they interconnected.
>
> She then arranged lots of one-on-one meetings with the many stakeholders she had identified. She had prepared a group of questions that she asked everyone (e.g. what tips would you give someone who had just joined the company?).
>
> Of course, after the meetings, she followed up with a thank-you note. For Amy, personal relationships are sacred and reciprocity

> nurtures them. The other person needs to see the value to him of investing his time. In the note, she also explained what the person concerned could expect from her.
>
> Obviously this was a continual process and she kept in contact with everyone.
>
> Over the years, Amy has realised that in some organisations the informal processes are more relevant than the formal ones. For instance, some important decisions might be made before a meeting that would involve all stakeholders. The meeting then becomes just a formal approval. In such cases, your network becomes extremely important, allowing your voice to be heard while the informal discussions take place.
>
> Amy's advice: Don't build a network for the sake of it. Be sincere about it and tell people what you can do for them. They have to see the value of their time investment.

Seek 'helping brains'

Asking for help will express recognition of your colleague's skills and value. Let your collaborator's boss know of his/her assistance.

Asking for help is also a good way to convert some of the staff you know into proper links in your network. It is not receiving help that is important. The importance lies in the genuine recognition of the other person's skills and value.

Look for 'helping brains' instead of 'helping hands'. In chapter *Be a helping hand* I recommended that you help in any way, even carrying heavy items. When asking for help, be tactful to ask for help that requires knowledge, not just physical strength. You want to recognize the other person's knowledge, not physical abilities.

Imagine that in order to write a strategy paper for your vice-president you require some knowledge of manufacturing in Brazil. During your exploration of the corporation (see chapter *Move around the corporation*) you met someone who has just returned from an assignment in Brazil. You will contact this person again and ask for her advice or expertise. When you discuss the matter with her ensure that you know who assigned her to the Brazilian project.

Your strategy paper should include an acknowledgements section. Ensure you recognize your colleague's collaboration. Once you have finalized it and sent it to your vice-president, you should also send a copy to:

- Your colleague, including a thank you note, and maybe a token of appreciation such as small chocolates that she can share with peers.
- Your colleague's boss, including a note describing how valuable her input has been.
- The person who assigned her to Brazil, including a note explaining that the Brazilian assignment had an added benefit through the input into the strategy paper.

What you are doing is more than telling your colleague that you appreciate her knowledge. You are doing so in front of peers and managers. Sending a thank-you note only to your colleague would not be sufficient.

Let me explore the importance of public recognition with another example. In order to achieve some minor task, a colleague from your department points you towards the right person within the marketing area. That person is instrumental in your completing that task. Even if it was a minor task, ensure that you publicly thank your colleague during the next weekly meeting. You do not need to go on at length describing your task. The following would suffice: 'Let me thank John for introducing me to the person who helped me finish our promotion poster.' It is a short sentence that makes your colleague shine in front of the rest of the department. Forget about yourself and let your colleague shine. He was instrumental in your achieving the task. He deserves the spotlight.

> **Case Study: Martin Varsavsky**
>
> (CEO and Co-Founder, Fon)
>
> For over twenty-five years Martin Varsavsky has been an insatiable serial entrepreneur. He has founded companies in very different sectors, from biotechnology to telecommunications, and many more.
>
> When Martin has a new idea, he takes three major steps:
>
> 1. He employs an industry expert, someone who is a leader respected in that industry.
> 2. He studies everything on that subject. In some cases, he enrols in university courses and, in other cases, he hires personal tutors.
> 3. He analyzes the market. He travels worldwide to see where there will be the minimum initial resistance to the concept that he is developing.
>
> Martin gives an example of the first step when he founded a company that renovated lofts in Manhattan. In that case he employed the former New York City real estate commissioner. Martin had the flair to find great locations but lacked the personal connections to secure funding. The expert whom he recruited brought such connections into the venture.
>
> Let's note that Martin does not network actively. For him the contacts come after gaining authority on a subject. 'If you have something to say and others are interested, the contacts will

> come on their own.' To Martin the value of your contribution in a field is more important than the contacts that you may have.
>
> Martin's advice: when you start a company, employ an expert with experience and contacts.

Maintaining

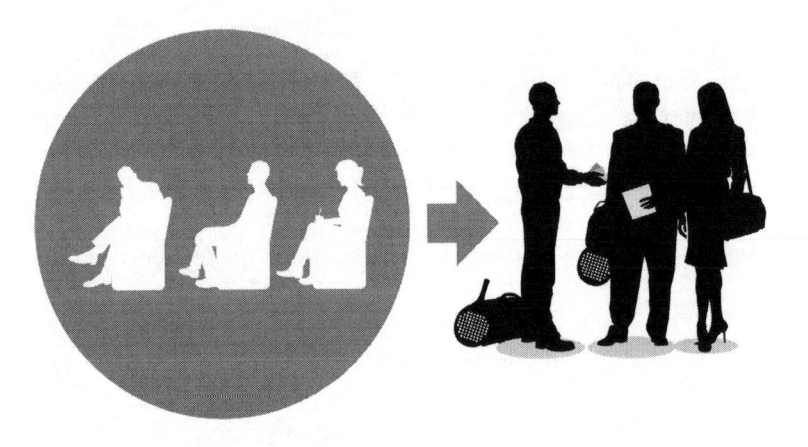

Add value. Share your contacts. Engage in informal shared activities.

Bring back value to your colleagues

Before, during and after the conference look out for ways to bring value back to your colleagues.

Before the conference

When you are planning to attend a conference, think how that conference could be of benefit to some of your colleagues. Think broadly. Think further than your department. Think corporation.

You should inform your colleagues that you are attending the conference and that you have identified something of benefit to them. It can be a session, a particular speaker or even a participant you have noticed in the attendees list. You want to clarify what you could do that your colleague would value, for instance you could:

- Attend a particular session in order to ask a specific question.
- Give your colleague's business card to a particular speaker.
- Arrange a meeting between your colleague and a particular participant.
- Contact the organizers on behalf of your colleague.
- Talk informally about a particular issue to the commentators and media people.

When contacting your colleague take care of your language. It could sabotage your best intentions. Do not say, 'I'm off to Palm Springs for the ABC Conference. You would love the final session because...' Instead you could say, 'The ABC Conference is next week. I will attend the final session as I could bring back valuable information to you because...' The difference is obvious. The former focuses on the destination and points out how unlucky your colleague is. The latter focuses on the conference and the benefit you can bring back to your colleague.

During the conference

During the conference keep in mind your colleagues' requests. You might even inform each of them about the progress. For instance you can send short emails or text messages such as, 'Met X from Company Y. He'll phone you to schedule meeting.' Doing so will make very clear to your colleagues that you really meant to get some value back to them.

At the event, you will meet people you didn't expect to meet, or learn about things you didn't expect to learn. In such cases, ask yourself who, within the corporation, could benefit from that contact or knowledge.

After the conference

When you get back from the conference, produce a short document with your notes from the conference. You can share it during your regular department meeting. In addition to storing the document in your department document repository, you can also distribute the document to the colleagues who can benefit from it. When you give or send the document, include any relevant items collected at the conference, such as copies of one or more business cards, relevant leaflets, articles, and samples.

You should distribute the document to a broader circle than just the colleagues who requested something from the conference. Include anyone who could benefit from the unexpected meetings or from learning about what happened during the event.

After you have practiced this a couple of times you will notice that your colleagues might come to you with requests as soon as they know you are attending a conference. This will be proof that your strategy was valuable to the corporation.

Add your contacts to the corporation's network

Select contacts in your address book that would bring value to your corporation. Add them to the corporations' address book.
Notify the colleagues who would benefit from them.

You have many contacts outside the corporation. Should you give them to the corporation? Wouldn't you lose value because the rest of the corporation will contact them, bypassing you?

The answer, as usual, comes from looking at it from the other side. Which choice will be of benefit to your colleagues? The answer is obvious you should add your contacts.

Do not worry about the rest of the staff contacting them. Your links with these people will not lose strength. Most probably they will become stronger. Indeed, a networking link is more than a name and a phone number. It involves the trust that you have built up during the many interactions with that person. In addition, if your contacts gain value when your colleagues contact them, they will remember you as the reason for their relationship. The better their relationship is, the higher you will be in their 'ranking of contacts'.

Of course, you shouldn't just copy your entire address book into the corporate customer relationship management (CRM) system. You need to be selective and only add the entries that will provide value to your colleagues and to the organization as a whole. If the system has a space for comments, you can add your name as the person who entered it into the system. This will allow the rest of the staff to contact you if they need more information about that person. At the same time, it offers you some extra visibility within the corporation.

While you are identifying the entries that you will include in the corporation network, you should also determine who within the corporation could benefit from it. You ought to let those staff members know that you have added those particular contacts and why they might benefit. Ideally you should send individual messages to each of them in order to identify which of those new contacts could be of interest to them.

You will be replicating the old story of the farmer who helped the neighbouring fields pollinate his own field. That farmer won the state competition in the corn category five times in a row. His secret was to give his award-winning corn to his neighbours. Since corn is pollinated from surrounding fields, he understood that he could only have top corn if his neighbours had very good corn[4].

Be generous when pollinating your corporation's network!

Develop trust through informal shared activities

Seek activities you can share. If the activities evoke passion in your colleagues and they have something at stake, this will help develop trust.

A very good place to develop trust between two individuals is during recurrent informal activities that are of interest to both of them.

This is what Brian Uzzi and Shannon Dunlap, professors at the Kellogg School of Management, call the 'shared activities principle' in a recent *Harvard Business Review* article. They claim that, 'Potent networks are not forged through casual interactions but through relatively high-stakes activities that connect you with diverse others.' During shared activities you freely interact with others. Unscripted behaviours, as opposed to prescribed business roles, allow the interaction to be more genuine. Thus, you have the proper ground for trust creation and growth.

---

4 'Whoopee in the Cornfields', Networking Entrepreneur blog by Ivan Misner. http://networking.entrepreneur.com/2010/05/24/whoopee-in-the-cornfields/ (accessed 3 June 2010).

Shared activities come in many shapes and forms, such as sports teams, community service ventures, interdepartmental initiatives, voluntary associations, and cross-functional teams. However, not all shared activities are equally potent regarding the creation of strong networks. The best activities are those that:

- Evoke passion,
- Need interdependence, and
- Have something at stake.

It is not just a matter of doing the same activity as the other person. The stakes must be high for both of you. For instance, you might like running in the park early in the morning. The marketing vice-president of your new corporation happens to run in the same park every morning. After a few days you might start saying hello to each other. However, there is nothing at stake. You are not sharing an activity. You are only doing the same independent activity in the same park at the same time of day. That's it.

Now compare the previous case to the following example. You join the corporation's rowing team (or other group sport). After a while there, you will be sharing more than just a 'Good morning, sir'. The best part will be when you compete at a tournament (even if local). You will share the goal: achieving the best position for your team. There is something at stake. And something public as the local newspaper might even publish a story about it.

With shared activities you will be avoiding the 'surface networker syndrome'. Researchers from the University of Virginia and Accenture describe it: 'The surface networker engages in surface-level interactions to connect with others but does not engage in behaviours that build the personal connection, sense of trust and reciprocity critical to relationships that are truly helpful over time.'

You will find many surface networkers at social networking websites. They are professionals with breadth but not depth. They have huge amounts of links in their online networks (LinkedIn, Facebook or other). However, they have rarely interacted with them, let alone provided them with something valuable.

As Liz Lynch writes in her book *Smart Networking*, 'The secret lies less in who's in your network and more in how you relate to your network'.

PART 2

Network in a New Industry

Are you looking to start in a new industry? Are you looking for a career change? Have you recently changed industry?

If you answered 'yes' to any of the previous questions, networking will help you to be successful in your new occupation.

Industry changes can be very diverse. Some executives change into very different sectors. For instance, Martha Stewart left a successful career as stockbroker on Wall Street to start a catering company. Jeff Bezos abandoned his banking career to found Amazon.

In particular, if you are leaving academia to start a new venture, study this part of the book. You can build great technology. However, your venture needs the right contacts outside your technical domain in order to succeed. Research by Professors Indre Maurer and Mark Ebers (Universtiy of Cologne) found that 'the less successful [new enterprises] continued to esteem and concentrate on their relations within the scientific community....The more successful [ones], however, intensified and strengthened some of their newly formed relationships.'

Surveying your new industry

Speak the industry's language. Subscribe to trade magazines.

Speak the industry's language

Get to know the acronyms, phrases, twists and different meanings used in your new industry.

Learning the jargon or language of your new industry should be one of your first objectives. An industry's language includes things such as acronyms, phrases, twists, and of course, different meanings for the same word.

Depending on the industry, you can find a dictionary on that industry's lingo. For instance, if you were moving into a real estate profession you might want to buy the relevant *Barron's Business Guide (Dictionary of Real Estate Terms)*. Even when you are able to find a relevant dictionary, you should do more than browse it to build your industry language. For instance, you could:

- Watch interviews of industry leaders.
- Read newsletters and trade magazines (see also chapter *Subscribe to trade magazines*).
- Attend conferences.
- Schedule a conversation with someone within your network who is working in that industry.

Newsletters and blog posts might use language closer to the spoken language. This might make them more useful to your endeavour than trade magazines. However, trade magazines will be most helpful when they define particular terms, either as a footnote or within the article. Thus, it might be a good approach to read formal and informal publications, as you will obtain valuable industry language information from both.

When attending conferences, do not hesitate to ask informally for clarification of terms used by the speakers. You can do so during coffee breaks with people with whom you feel comfortable. An even better approach would be to befriend a journalist attending the conference. They are highly qualified to clarify industry jargon.

The ideal location for one-to-one meetings is where other people from that industry normally gather. For instance, it can be a coffee shop in an area with several companies belonging to that industry. This will allow you also to feel (and breathe) the industry culture. How do the people dress? How do they interact with each other?

What do you see in terms of their body language?

Unfortunately before moving from academia into a telecommunications carrier, I didn't learn the industry jargon. Why should I? I thought that my telecommunications engineering degree and my PhD had taught me everything I needed to know about the telecommunications language. It didn't even occur to me that I had to learn terminology and acronyms.

During my first month in the job, I attended all the meetings and internal seminars I could (see also chapter *Make yourself even more visible via larger groups*). I felt they were talking a different language! Someone said, 'We need to improve our SLAs'. Someone replied, 'We already have five-nines!' I didn't know what an SLA was but I knew what a nine was. My little brain thought that 'five-nines' meant that five customers had rated us nine out of ten. Nothing was further from reality. Five-nines means that the systems are working properly 99.999% of the time! I hadn't surveyed the new industry properly. I required extra catch-up, which I did by talking to my colleagues.

Case Study: Gary Linnane

(Australian Broadcasting Corporation,
Board of Directors Secretary)

Gary has worked in the Australia public service since 1972. His career has comprised senior roles in many departments and public corporations.

He rejoined the ABC (Australian Broadcasting Corporation) in 1995, having had a two-year term three years before that as senior adviser to the managing director. From 1995 he worked in several senior corporate roles until being appointed chief of staff in the managing director's office. He then worked in this capacity for three managing directors. Networking was very easy for him because he was working directly for the top executive of the corporation. After the weekly meetings of senior managers, he had to follow up all of them. This enabled him to have contacts in every division.

After starting the job, he read lots of different industry publications and internal reports. He did ask lots of questions and listened intensively to what people had to say. Such efforts helped him to understand how the industry works as well as to familiarise himself with the terminology. He makes the point of the great effort and time he required to understand the so-called 'ratings system'.

At meetings, if he didn't understand something, he did not interrupt to ask for clarification. Instead, he followed up later with the relevant people. This way he had a better clarification and, in addition, he established rapport with the other person.

He understood that most organisations tend to be factionalised. For that reason, before he could be labelled as belonging to one faction or another, he took every opportunity to establish relationships with people. He seized opportunities as they arose.

The other employees didn't see him as a threat. They wanted him to understand their position. So he made an early impression on each person and moved quickly to the next one.

Gary's advice is: 'You have two ears and one mouth. Use them in that proportion'.

Subscribe to trade magazines

Regularly reading trade magazines will provide you with useful information and insights.

Your new industry might seem to be uncharted territory to you. You are right. There are no comprehensive charts or maps for that industry. However, trade magazines can serve you as good resources.

You should subscribe to the magazines and not just buy one every now and then. You will receive them regularly. You will see changes happening in the industry. You will start 'feeling' that industry.

For starters, trade magazines will help you learn the industry's language (see chapter *Speak the industry's language*). In addition, you will know who are the top players and key people in that industry. You will even be interested in the advertisements, which are a way to know the industry players. They will help you discover niche companies that you didn't even know existed. You will learn about up-coming conferences or even read about past ones. You might even want to write some articles for them (as discussed in chapter *Write articles in trade magazines*).

Some trade magazines offer added value to subscribers. For instance, you might be able to attend receptions and events that are for subscribers only. If this is the case, be sure you attend such events. In addition to meeting people from your industry you might get to know the magazine editors. They are often a source of great advice and contacts.

Should the magazines run a survey or poll, be sure you complete it. Often magazines draw a prize for the respondents. It will give you the chance not just to win a prize but also to have your name in front of all the subscribers when the magazine publishes the names of the winners.

Regularly reading trade magazines will provide you with a great source of information that might also be valuable to your previous industry, as we will see in chapter *Develop bridges with your previous industries*.

Building

Be active at conferences. Phone, meet and phone. Write articles.

Reactivate old connections and cultivate more 'weak ties'

Actively seek recommendations from previous relationships.

Some of your connections might be an excellent gateway to great people in your new industry. You should reactivate the contact with them.

You can follow these steps:

1. Notify some of your contacts that you are now in the new industry (or that you want to move into it). You should mention that, in order to better understand it, you would like to get their recommendations of people worth contacting within your new industry. Let's use the term 'advisers' for the ones that volunteer contacts (see chapter *Growing your network, one node at a time*).
2. For some of those recommendations, your advisers have allowed you to mention their name during your conversation. Make contact with them. In practice, you can forget about the rest of recommended names, as contacting them would be essentially a simple cold call.
3. You thank each adviser after having made the recommended contacts (see chapter *The magic of 'thank you'*).

You might not receive recommendations soon after your notification. However, you have reactivated some old connections. In the coming days, some of them might come across someone they could recommend to you. Thanks to your recent notification you will be on their minds. Don't be surprised if someone gets back to you a few weeks later saying something along the lines, 'Yesterday I happened to meet Mr. Bloggs and he would be interested in knowing more about your plans in the new industry.'

You will also know about relevant industry people through trade journals (see chapter *Speak the industry's language*). You should try to contact the most relevant ones. Relevance is according to your own objective, not to rank or to status. For instance, a marketing director might be more relevant to your network than a CEO.

You can use online tools, such as LinkedIn, to investigate whether those relevant people are in your extended network. For example, suppose that John wants to contact Angie who is a communications vice-president. John searches for Angie in LinkedIn and discovers that his previous boss, Kate, used to work with Angie. John then phones Kate to catch up and to ask for an introduction to Angie. After that catch-up, he phones Angie. In his first sentence he mentions that Kate suggested that phone call. Using the steps mentioned above, instead of just cold calling, John multiplies by a factor of twenty the chances of achieving a contact with Angie.

Notice the following from the previous example:

- Online tools (such as LinkedIn) are best used to gather information about people but not to contact them.
- The phone is the preferred method for the first contact (see chapter *To speak or to write?*).

Don't be just an attendee at conferences

Arrive early at conferences, ask questions to gain visibility and make the most of the coffee breaks. Schedule time for following up.

You cannot just attend conferences. You must participate in them.

To attend a conference is just a matter of sitting through the sessions and listening to the speakers. To participate in a conference requires being active.

Prepare for the conference

You've identified a great conference to attend. Great! But hold

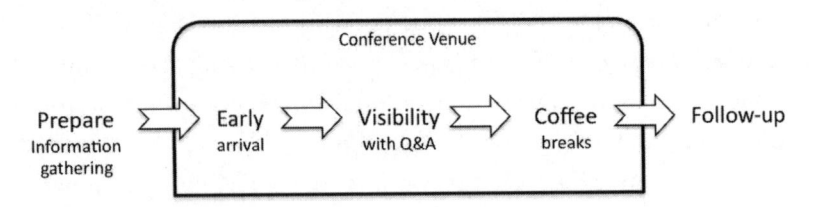

Prepare (Information gathering) → Early arrival → Visibility with Q&A → Coffee breaks → Follow-up [Conference Venue]

Attending conferences is much more than showing up at the event.

on there are lots of things to do before you arrive at the venue. Jan Vermeiren, in his book *Let's Connect*, gives some examples:

- You should register early so that you appear in all the attendees' lists.
- If there is an official hotel for the conference, book a room there. It will be a great way to bump into speakers and organisers.
- You can contact the speakers who are relevant to your goal. Let them know that you will be at the conference and would like to discuss a particular topic.
- You should get the list of attendees. You can identify relevant ones and contact them. You might find that some people in your network are attending the conference. It will be a great opportunity to catch up with them.
- You should examine the program to identify the sessions you will attend.
- You should adapt your self-introduction to this conference (see chapter *Your self-introduction: a memorable single sentence*).

One last thing before you go: remind yourself of what you will try to achieve at the conference.

Arrive early

You should arrive early at the conference venue so you can:

- Talk to the speakers as they arrive.
- Confer with other attendees whom you identified during the preparation.
- Get to know the organisers (they are often well-connected people).
- Practice and refine your self-introduction.
- Help other participants when they arrive and need some orientation. You will be of benefit to those participants and they will remember you.

You should also identify the room where the first session takes place. Familiarise yourself with this room. This will reduce your apprehension about asking a question, as suggested below.

Ask a question

Most participants will attend the first session of a conference, often a plenary with one or more keynote speakers. What is more important than listening to the speakers? It's asking a question that everyone will listen to!

And even better, they will listen to your single-sentence self-introduction (see chapter *Your self-introduction: a memorable single sentence*) at the beginning of the question. The idea is to make yourself visible to the rest of the attendees and even to the star speaker. This is extremely useful when you are new to the industry.

During the session you should think about potential questions relevant to the lecture. When the speaker finishes, the questions & answers part usually begins. Then:

- You raise your hand.
- Your heart starts pumping faster and faster.

- You take deep breaths while someone brings the microphone to you.
- You stand up and smile.
- You state clearly your single-sentence self-introduction.
- You might even (very briefly) communicate your reason for attending the conference.
- You ask an intelligent, sharp and short question.
- You smile and listen attentively to the answer.
- You have just gained visibility with the rest of attendees. Well done!

Attend the breaks

Your preferred session should be the coffee break.

At breaks, meals and cocktails you will be able to talk to people in a more relaxed environment than in the workplace. Susan RoAne authored a book about this called *How to Work a Room*.

Coffee breaks can be scary, in particular when you are at a conference in new territory. Such insecurity might tempt you to phone your office to check that everything is fine. The time allocated for the coffee break can easily slip by. Don't do it! Make the most of coffee break time.

In all the coffee breaks that I have attended, there was at least one person even more scared than me. You're not alone!

A good starting point will be to approach people who are standing alone, probably because they are intimidated by the thought of approaching other people. You first tell them your self-introduction (see chapter *Your self-introduction: a memorable single sentence*), you ask them about the conference, and then the dialogue starts.

You should not get into a formal work discussion. Your main objective during the breaks should be to have brief discussions with people in order to:

- Let them know how you can help them.
- Assess if you want to meet them again to develop the contact.
- If so, exchange contact information and propose a follow-up meeting in the coming days.
- Then you move on to meet other people.

Once you are confident with this *modus operandi*, you will be able to approach groups of people. It is easier to approach groups (three or more people) than pairs, especially if their body language indicates they are open and may be having fun.

If you know someone in the group, approach that person and say hello. He or she will probably introduce you to the rest of the group. Otherwise, make eye contact with one of the group and stand next to that person. You can also introduce yourself to that person (only your name, no single-sentence self-introduction now). Then you listen to the conversation until you can contribute. At that moment, you speak; of course, ensuring that you do not interrupt anyone else, just wait for that little silence. You want to melt into the conversation; don't try to steer it towards your personal topics of interest.

Schedule the follow-up

Most likely, on the first day back at the office you'll be swamped by the many tasks that are waiting for you. So you might decide to postpone the follow-up with all those new contacts. Tomorrow will surely be easier. However, tomorrow arrives and you're back into the office routine and urgent matters arise. So you postpone those follow-ups for one more day. You can imagine the never-ending story of tomorrows and deferments.

A proven way out of this spiral is never to get into it. When you plan a conference in your diary, you should include some time for follow-ups during the subsequent days. For instance, you could schedule follow-ups from 9am to 11am for the two days after the conference.

If it's not in your diary, it might not happen!

Become involved in associations

Join one or two associations and get really involved in them.

You need to do more than join the relevant professional associations in your new industry. You need to get involved in them.

Identifying the relevant association in your industry should be easy. If it is not, try to locate a trade association that is somehow related to your industry. Suppose that you are the general manager of a toy factory in a remote Brazilian town. There might be no associations of factory managers in that region. However, you might join the regional association of corporate executives, the local chamber of commerce, or the Rotary Club.

An association might look very good on paper and be a very different thing in reality. It is worth your while to attend one or two meetings before joining the association (see also chapter *Join the right clubs*). However, once you join the association, you should get involved in its operations. You don't need to run for president to be of benefit to its membership. You can:

- Volunteer for one of the committees that might be in place.
- Help with the regular events. It can be as simple as turning up a half-hour before the event starts and helping set up the chairs in the room.
- Assist with their publications. You can put newsletters into envelopes or even help with the production of the newsletter.

What you are actually doing is having a shared activity with people in your industry (see chapter *Develop trust through informal shared activities*). However, don't over-commit to too many associations. It is usually better to get fully involved in one or two associations than to be only slightly involved in lots of associations.

The advice in chapter *Don't be just an attendee at conferences* applies to the associations' events too. In particular, arriving early will prove most useful. It will allow you to meet other members. You will also gather information on ways you can help the association.

Most associations have regular events. Some are weekly events. Others are monthly events. You should make the effort to attend most regular events during your first months in the association. This will not only help you gain visibility with other members but also to better understand the association's activities, and you will be in a much better position to ascertain how you can best help the association.

Case Study: David McLellan

(Managing Director APAC, Triscreen Media Group)

David started moving across borders at a very early age. As a child he lived in three different countries with his parents—the United Kingdom, Spain and Denmark. Thus it is no surprise that he has continued moving countries during his career.

In June 1983 his Danish employer sent him to Barcelona to develop the company's southern European business.
In 1984 David moved to Australia where he took several senior executive roles.
In 1990 he moved back to Europe where he took a senior role in Madrid.
After four years he moved back to Australia where he has worked ever since.

Only once did he join an expat club, and then out of curiosity. He found that the club was closed in around itself with very few links to the local community. This is what David explains about expat communities, 'They tend to be a good place to get started, particularly if you don't speak the language. However, the people that join often get trapped among themselves!'

Every single time David moved to a new country, he joined the local bridge and tennis clubs. He usually went even further and joined the club committee. He became really involved in the club's life.

David joins the right associations even if he doesn't move to the country. During a number of years he spent half of his time in Australia and the other half in California (establishing a subsidiary company for his employer). While there he joined a Californian bridge club and the California Tennis Association.

The main reason David joins the local clubs is that he loves bridge and tennis. It is the best place to play them. The added benefit is that these activities attract 'high-end people' who fill the clubs with great networking opportunities.

Write articles in trade magazines

Writing articles in trade magazines will be a gateway to valuable contacts in your new industry.

If you can read trade magazines, you should also write for them.

Writing articles in trade magazines will bring many benefits, including:

- Making your name known in the industry.
- Knowing key people from that industry.
- Helping you understand the main issues that the industry is facing.

You might remember how hard it was for you to complete essays at university. Just the memory of the rigid reference system makes you shiver. However, writing for a trade magazine is simpler. Normally you don't need to adhere to a pre-established reference system. Quoting other authors becomes much easier.

There are lots of things that you can write about that can be of interest to the readers. Magazines are often hungry for articles. If you are short on ideas, you can talk to the magazine editor. You can explain your degrees, interests and previous jobs. Ask the editor about the three most burning issues for their readers. Most probably the editor will suggest a topic for your article or series of articles. You will not only discover potential topics, you will also gain an excellent contact for your network: the editor.

The pretext of an article will provide excellent ground to interview the key actors in the industry. It is much easier to talk to CEOs when the objective is to write an article than when the objective is to look for a job! The interview should be short around twenty minutes. You don't need to publish the full interview. It will be the raw material that will provide you with quotes to support the claims in your article.

Should you write a single article or a series of articles? Do what you are capable of doing. You should feel comfortable with the format you will be using. Otherwise your articles will come across as forced. Your articles should genuinely show your way of thinking.

Phone, meet, and phone again!

Phone to schedule meetings at which you will build trust.

You have met lots of new people at conferences and working groups (see chapters *Don't be just an attendee at conferences* and *Become involved in associations*). You want to develop trust with as many of them as possible. Trust will convert some of them from contacts to network links.

You are not known (or at least not yet!) in your new industry. Therefore you will need to use the tools most appropriate to build trust. The face-to-face meeting is the best tool (see chapter *To speak or to write?*). Your facial expressions and eye contact will be the raw materials to build the other person's trust.

Speaking over the telephone is a good option when meeting in person is not feasible. Your voice and its tone can also help build trust little by little.

Email is not a trust-building tool: it is a good asynchronous[5] working tool. Remember that the brain areas that deal with trust are its most

---

5 'Asynchronous' denotes a system in which the people do not need to communicate at the very same time.

primitive areas. They work the same way as they used to work when humans lived in caves. They become active with human contact. Email cannot easily activate them.

With some of your new contacts, you may have already scheduled a follow-up appointment at your first meeting. With others you need to get that meeting. In those cases, you will:

- Phone the person.
- Remind him or her about your recent conversation and reiterate your self-introduction.
- Evoke the topic of mutual interest you agreed to discuss further.
- Propose a couple of dates to meet.
- Stop talking and start listening.

More often than not, you will agree right there and then on a time and place to meet. However, if the other person is reluctant to meet, do not force the meeting to happen. Instead, have a brief discussion over the phone. As usual, you should follow up the brief discussion with a brief email or handwritten thank-you note.

You should use any opportunity to put your voice and tone in front of other industry people and stakeholders. For instance, the following are situations where you should do it:

- When sending an article, you can telephone and explain to the other person why you thought of him or her when reading the article.
- When passing on a 'hello' from a common acquaintance.
- When thanking people after meeting the person they recommended.

'Who do you recommend I speak to?' is a great question to ask, either in person or over the phone. Asking the same question via email doesn't have the potential for interactivity and quite often you will not get a recommendation. In person or over the phone you can make suggestions such as, 'What about someone in a cross-sectional marketing department?' Such questions might trigger new recommendations from the other person.

When somebody recommends that you meet someone, you should meet that person even if you think it will be a waste of time for both of you. You might be right but, among other things, you are building trust with the recommending person. You must show appreciation for the advice. After meeting that person, you will phone the recommending person to let him or her know about the meeting. By doing so, you will increase, even if only slightly, the trust with that person and in addition you can prompt for new recommendations.

Case Study: Chris Golis

(Author and professional speaker on
Practical Emotional Intelligence)

By 1979 Chris had been working in the information technology (IT) industry for more than thirteen years and needed a change. He realised he was in a mid-life crisis and was wondering what to do.

The book *'The Manager's Guide to Successful Job Hunting'* by Robert G. Traxel inspired him to take action. Traxel argues that the best way to solve a mid-life crisis is to change careers, and recommends a seven-step plan, which Chris followed assiduously. The fourth step was 'Interview CEOs in your target industry'. The following is an excerpt of what Chris explains about his experience.

Step 1. Goal Setting (Set a date nine months away when you will accept your position)

Step 2. Discover who you are (Establish your strengths, weaknesses and skill levels)

Step 3. Verify whether you can do the job

Step 4. Carry out the preliminary interviews

Meet with the CEOs of the top twenty companies in the industry you have targeted. My telephone cold call went like this:

'I need your help. I am a graduate of the London Business School and currently a divisional general manager with TNT. A graduate I recently hired suggested that I consider a career as an investment banker. May I have twenty minutes of your time to discuss whether this is a good idea?'

Not one CEO refused an interview. After I thanked them for granting me an interview, I said I was carrying out a survey of twenty leaders in the industry and would ask two key questions:

- You are obviously a success in your industry; what are the three reasons why you think you succeeded?
- Of all your competitors, which are the three you most respect?

This information is most useful but the most important thing is not to make the mistake of talking about yourself. When the conversation inevitably turns to the CEO asking you to describe who you are, you politely say that you have not made the decision to join the industry and that will only come when you complete the survey. Instead, you thank them for their time, and gracefully leave, and write them a short letter expressing gratitude for the meeting. Traxel says that if you do that they will never forget you. If instead you take the opportunity to describe yourself you destroy your authenticity. My own personal experience totally vindicated Traxel's argument. The one interview where I broke his 'no talking about yourself' rule turned into a disaster.

All the other CEOs whom I met subsequently at industry functions all came rushing up to me saying how they never forgot that interview. All had worked out what I was doing, and every one of them said, *'You know, if I were going to switch careers I would have used your approach.'*

Step 5. Draw up your product profile

You now have a list of the strengths you need to be successful. You then write a letter along the following lines:

'I have completed my survey. I have concluded that there are seven characteristics you need to be a successful investment banker.' And then you list the seven. You then conclude your letter by saying, *'If you look at my enclosed CV by some coincidence you will see I have all seven characteristics. I will telephone you next week to arrange a meeting.'*

Step 6. Send off the letters and start the interviews

Step 7. Accept an offer on the date you set nine months ago in Step 1!!

The interviews carried out at step four gave Chris great visibility

> and recognition within the industry. This was extremely useful later on, for instance, to get articles about his career published in leading business magazines.
>
> Chris says now that he would check his fitness for a job by using an organisational psychologist. Otherwise the secret is to follow diligently a proven method like the one thirty years ago [referring to Traxel's book].

Prepare even harder before every meeting

Look for ways to give value to the person you will be meeting.

You must prepare even harder before meeting someone. You will arrange meetings with people in order to achieve multiple goals. Thus, you need to prepare extensively.

My favourite university professor told me that she normally spent four hours preparing for a one-hour lecture. You should do the same. Even if you plan to meet someone for twenty minutes, spend at least an hour and a half preparing for it. Your preparation before meeting an individual should provide answers to the following questions:

- How can you help that person? What are their current or recent challenges? You will gather background information on that person to get potential ideas. If you cannot come up with a straightforward way to help, you will have gathered information that will be very useful when you 'listen between the lines' at the meeting.
- What information from your previous industries might they be interested in? As described in chapter *Develop bridges with your previous industries* you cannot discard your connections in your previous industries. They can be a great plus in your trust building efforts.

- Who can this person refer you to? You can use online tools such as LinkedIn to investigate if that person knows someone you would like to speak to. You can also find potential acquaintances by looking into his board memberships (present or past), positions held or even participation in associations.

Your meeting's preparation will also provide information about your new industry. It is easier to read documentation, articles or books when you have a clear objective. Such preparation will be a very useful objective. It is much harder when you are reading just to get educated on your new industry. You can kill two birds with one stone: prepare for the meeting and get information on the industry.

Your preparations can go further than looking for information. Don't hesitate to find some item that can be of use to the other person. The obvious items are informational ones, such as an article or a book. However, if you know that the other person is passionate about something, find a rare object related to that passion. Executives' interests come in many shapes and forms such as golf, professional sports, stamps, coins or model cars. You can also default to a newspaper of a date relevant to the other person (birth, graduation, or retirement).

Maintaining

Be patient. Build bridges between industries.

Don't rush

Do not rush. Establishing trust takes time!

Maintaining useful links in the network takes time. There are no shortcuts. Moving too fast could even destroy some trust.

Pino Bethencourt, a Spanish networking expert, puts it very clearly when she writes that 'networking requires a certain interaction pace.' Your road network will not run better if you rush its construction. On the contrary, cracks might appear in the future if the foundations were not sound. Networking needs a certain amount of interaction at regular intervals. Do not try to force such intervals into happening sooner.

The following is an example of such patience. Suppose that in order to arrange a meeting, James phones Suzy, the mergers and acquisitions director of a financial corporation. Suzy has an extremely busy month. However, she has great appreciation for the person who recommended James to contact her. So she proposes either to meet the following day for a brief five or ten minutes, or alternatively to wait until next month and meet for a full hour. What should James do? Of course, he should wait until next month. Suzy can open many doors for James, or at least point out at which doors he should open. It will be a long wait until next month, but worth it. Ideally, during the phone conversation James should try to get a tentative date in the diary. Soon after the phone conversation James should write a follow-up email thanking Suzy for the brief phone conversation and stating the date agreed for a meeting. He can also send a brief reminder email a couple of days before the planned date.

The following is another example. Imagine that you have scheduled a meeting with Martin, a person very relevant to your networking objectives. You turn up at Martin's office and learn that he has completely forgotten about your meeting and is leaving for another appointment. This has happened to me many times! You are upset. However, you have probably gained some credit in your relationship with Martin and, of course, he now has a debit in his account with you. He will probably be sorry for the mix-up and will try to make up for it. Thus, he will probably be more helpful when you meet than he would have been at the initially planned meeting.

Thus, even if Martin proposes to meet briefly there and then, on the spot, politely decline. You have been waiting to meet Martin for so long. Now you are standing in front of him and could have a brief conversation with him. However, in Martin's mind that brief meeting might well write off the credit. You would not meet Martin again. Your best option is to reschedule the appointment, even if it will delay it by some days or weeks.

Develop bridges with your previous industries

Being the bridge for your contacts in two different industries is very valuable.

You nurture the links in your network, providing value to them. Can you offer any benefit when you are just starting in a new industry? Of course! Even more so, the fact that you come from another industry puts you in a unique position to add value.

There is a large amount of academic research in that area (academics call it 'structural holes'). One of the findings regarding networking between two industries is this: 'The more different the two industries, the more valuable a person who is connected to both industries becomes.'

Let's look at an example. Let's suppose that someone, we'll call him Matt, spent ten years working in the utilities sector. Last year he accepted an executive job in a big financial firm. Regarding his network bridges, he made many initiatives during the first six months on the job, among them:

- He put in contact the financial firm director and the operations manager from his previous utilities corporation. The former was in charge of assessing risk across industries. The latter was responsible for minimising operational risk.
- He summarised a few articles from a trade magazine he used to read in his previous industry. The articles gave advice to companies looking into acquiring their competitors. He then published those summaries in the leading mergers and acquisitions (M&A) magazine, read by most executives and vice-presidents of financial corporations.
- He organised a one-day seminar on a topic that was of interest to utilities and financial firms. He ensured that the speakers were well balanced across the two industries. He even planned a hands-on workshop where people from both industries formed teams. At the end of the day, everyone gained value from talking to people from the other industry. And Matt got all the credit for it.

If you make a move from the public to the private sector, or vice versa, you will also have many opportunities to build bridges between them. You will be in an excellent position to demystify half-truths from one side to the other.

After your industry change, most probably for some time you will keep receiving trade magazines from your previous industry. Do not discard them. Read them from your new perspective. Look out for articles or ideas that can be of use to someone in your new industry.

Case Study: Catherine DeVrye

(Author and professional speaker)

In 1992, after ten years in an executive role with IBM, Catherine saw an opportunity to do something she liked and started as a professional speaker.

She had built a good reputation while working at IBM. This reputation helped her get her first clients from her previous industry. Her initial speaking engagements were with clients from IT, banking and government. Through these initial bridges one thing led to another and she kept on growing her list of clients.

According to Catherine, your career is formed like building blocks. You don't want to make them tumble. You need to build the next level using the strengths of the current level. There are always exceptions to the rule but it is probably not wise to try something completely new that does not use any of the strengths from your previous job or profession.

Catherine's advice:

- Never burn your bridges with previous industries or companies, and
- Always play on your strengths.

PART 3

Networking Across a New Country

Are you intending to work in a new country? Have you already moved? Are you volunteering for an expat position within your current corporation? Or even, for reasons outside your control, have you found yourself living in another country? If you answered yes to any of these questions, you need advanced networking techniques to thrive in the new community.

Research from the Thunderbird School of Global Management, published by the *Harvard Business Review*, explains that to make it overseas you need a global mindset. This has three main components:

- Intellectual capital,
- Psychological capital, and
- Social capital.

Such a global mindset is developed early in life. Does this mean that you cannot succeed in another country if your parents didn't expose you to different cultures? Not at all! It just means that you need to make some extra effort to compensate. This section will help you to do so.

I have used the term 'country' throughout the book to mean 'geography' in the larger sense. The tips are most appropriate when you completely change country, culture and language. However, they are extremely useful when changing any one of these elements. For instance, someone moving from the French countryside into Paris will find the advice in this part of the book very useful. The term 'home country' denotes any previous countries you might have lived in. It is not restricted to the country where you were born.

Surveying

Explore the culture. Learn about current events.

Clarify your objective

A clear objective will help you meet the right people instead of just meeting lots of people.

Starting your network from scratch might seem daunting. You might feel compelled to increase the number of people in your network and meet the maximum number of people before and after going into the new country. This should not be your objective; it should be your means to get to your real objective.

You need to be very specific in your mind (and write it down on paper!). You should be very clear about why you need a network in your new country. Having specific written goals is instrumental in achieving such goals. A study by Gail Matthews at the Dominican University of California concludes, 'Those who wrote their goals accomplished significantly more than those who did not write their goals'[6].

Being very clear on your objective will guide your networking efforts. You will not waste your time and effort meeting lots of people. Instead you will put your effort into linking with the right people. Of course, linking goes much deeper than just meeting.

For example, among other objectives, you might need a network to:

- Feel comfortable and not miss your home country.
- Get new job opportunities.
- Employ people for your new venture.
- Develop sales channels for your company.

As you can see, the networking efforts will be very different in the examples given above. For instance, in order to feel comfortable you might want to join the expat association where people from your home country meet (see chapter *Join the right clubs*).

However, if you want to tap into new job opportunities you will network towards potential employers. They will most probably be board members and top executives. On the other hand, if you are trying to find employees, you will develop your contacts with people at the corresponding hierarchical levels in their organisations.

---

[6] Similar studies with Yale and Harvard students are often quoted. However, they seem to be an 'urban myth', see: http://faq.library.yale.edu/recordDetail?id=7508 (accessed 9th November 2010).

Learn about current events

Basic knowledge of current events will help you start conversations.

To build your network you will need some basic knowledge of the current events in your new country. It will be a must when starting conversations with people.

You should allocate a set amount of time every day to read about the current events in your new country. For instance, in the past I used to schedule twenty minutes every morning before leaving for work. If you haven't moved to the country yet, you can read online newspapers and blogs. You will not get as much as from reading a printed newspaper or watching the news on TV. However, you will be able to start grasping the local issues.

You can also plan on buying a different newspaper every day. Reading daily from a different source has the advantage of accessing a broader spectrum of facts and opinions. For instance, imagine that there are three main newspapers: *The Daily, The Times* and *The Reporter*. Each of them has a different political tendency and, thus, bias. You could allocate Mondays to *The Daily,* Tuesdays to *The Times,* Wednesdays to *The Reporter,* Thursday again to *The Daily* and so on. However, it is better not to have a day of the week allocated to a particular publication but rotate them instead. This will allow you to read the special sections newspapers often run on a particular day. For instance, *The Daily* might run the business news section on Wednesdays. If you had planned, for instance, to buy it on Tuesdays you would always miss that section.

All this reading will prove extremely helpful when you attend business events, which are always networking opportunities. During your first months in a new country, you may well be like a fish out of

The Daily, you buy it on:	Monday 1st	Thursday 4th	Sunday 7th	Wednesday 10th	Saturday 13th
The Times, you buy it on:	Tuesday 2nd	Friday 5th	Monday 8th	Thusday 11th	Sunday 14th
The Reporter, you buy it on:	Wednesday 3rd	Saturday 6th	Tuesday 9th	Friday 12th	Monday 15th

Example of rotating the newspaper that you buy each day.

water. You are not in your natural medium. By being conversant with current events, you will feel like a fish *in* water, even if not your usual water. In other words, you will gain comfort and thus be a better networker.

When it comes to topics for initiating conversation, weather, sports and politics are the usual suspects, together with the state of the economy. By reading about current events you will know about:

- How the current government is faring.
- What the main topics are for government and opposition.
- What the main sports that attract crowds are, and if they attract different social classes.
- How well the national teams are doing in international competitions.
- How the main economic indicators (unemployment-rate, inflation, etc.) are evolving.

Be careful when discussing politics. The person you are conversing with may hold a political belief that is unpopular. In addition, in some repressive countries it is unwise to mention politics at all. Be very careful and stick to non-controversial topics.

Explore the country's culture

To start networking it is essential to know the culture, which includes the office dress code, greetings, and professional rituals.

When you go into a new country you need basic language skills combined with a deep knowledge of the culture. Don't judge whether your culture handles situations better than your host country's culture. You are discovering the culture to maximise your networking efforts, not to change your new country's habits.

Knowing the basics of the language will remove some barriers when you start your networking efforts. In our road-building analogy, when you survey the terrain you will get better results by using the appropriate surveying instruments. It would be fantastic if you spoke their language fluently but, depending on your job, it might not be essential. However, if your role is an influencing one (e.g., business development) you will need an extensive knowledge of the language in order to penetrate the power structures.

Of course, knowing about its culture is also a sign of respect towards your host country. You should start your 'culture discovery' exercise before your move into the country. No matter how you approach it, it will be a never-ending exercise. You will keep discovering the country's culture by living there. Networking is based on developing trust among people. The cultural protocols used to develop trust can be very different from one country to another. Therefore it is crucial that you familiarise yourself with the culture.

For example, Asian cultures tend to have a collective focus while Western ones are more individualistic. Asians make sense of a new situation considering the context and the relations between stakeholders. Westerners, however, often observe the main object in the situation and apply a formal logical analysis. For instance, when meeting someone new, an Asian will focus on the common contacts between the two. However, a Westerner will focus on the person as an individual.

On the other hand, knowing the culture is really essential to start networking in your country. You need to know at least the minimum about:

- Dress code (relaxed or very formal).
- Greetings (shaking hands, bowing, or kisses).
- Addressing people (titles or first names).
- Eating rituals (such as not pouring your own drink in Japan).
- Working hours and time in the office (staying late in the office).

Getting information about culture is harder than about current events. However, you might find some published guides introducing the culture of your new country[7]. You can also get valuable information from websites aimed at expatriates[8]. However, do not be fooled into reading the introduction of a travel guide. It will cover topics of interest to the traveller. The topics that you need to know most probably will not be covered.

There are fine cultural differences that relate to how people network in different cultures. The more you can discover about them, the better you will be equipped. Standard stereotypes exist, such as:

---

7 For instance: [1] Explorer Publishing specialises in books written from a local perspective and aimed at the new resident; with a particular focus on Middle Eastern countries (see: www.explorerpublishing.com); and [2] Marshall Cavendish publishes the collection 'Culture Shock' (see: http://www.amazon.com/gp/search/ref=sr_adv_b/?search-alias=stripbooks&field-title=culture+shock&field-publisher=marshall+cavendish).
8 For instance: www.expatexchange.com

French are rigid about organisational structures, Chinese prioritise group interests, Japanese try not to stand out, and Argentineans have fluid boundaries between work and pleasure. However, you have to learn more than the old clichés.

Research from the University of Chicago (published in *Organization Science*) reveals that American managers hold a different approach to networking than French managers. French managers build relationships in a way distinct from the Americans. 'The French are anchored in long-standing personal relationships to which they add recent acquaintances from work. The Americans are anchored in long-standing work relations to whom they add personal relations with recent acquaintances.' For instance, American managers tend to know more of their current colleagues before joining the firm than French managers do. French managers are more resistant to having 'bridge relationships', that is, linkages with people from outside their organisation.

However, you can use your differences to your advantage, as shown in the following example.

Let's assume that Josh is an American executive who has just moved to Paris on a five-year assignment. Josh has done his work on discovering the culture. He is aware of the tendency of French managers not to pursue linkages outside of their corporation. Should he stop any networking outside his firm? No, he shouldn't, because he is also aware that even if French managers don't do it, they do not feel bad about other executives doing it. Thus Josh will keep on networking outside his corporation. He will even be glad to know that he has little competition for it because most French managers will not do it.

What if your culture discovery efforts lead you to the conclusion that in your host country networking is not used? You might need to dig deeper. As INSEAD's Organizational Behavior Professor, Herminia Ibarra, points out, 'I haven't seen any national culture (in which) things don't get done through networks.' During the last year I heard the following comments:

- A North American: 'Southern Europeans are better than us at networking as they are more prone to talk to strangers at social parties or at the local coffee shop.'
- An Italian: 'The Brits are better than us at networking because they have it formalised with their networking functions.'
- A Brit: 'The people from the USA are better than us at networking on account of their outgoing nature. They have networking in their blood!'

So get over all those cultural clichés and forget about excuses not to network. Instead you should get the maximum of intercultural empathy. The research dean at the Thunderbird School of Global Management, Mansour Javidan, offers some tips on building your plan to increase your social capital. You need to approach it in a methodical and prepared way. Otherwise it might not happen in the long run. One of the tips is to 'widen your circle of social interaction to include individuals with interests that diverge from yours.'

From my personal experience, this needs to go much further than having lunch with someone from a different culture. You can engage in a shared activity with that individual. To be effective that activity should evoke passion and have high stakes (see chapter *Develop trust through informal shared activities*). I once used a weekly tennis session as shared activity with an individual. During the tennis exchanges we didn't converse much. However, we were implicitly building trust. This appeared very clear to me from the informal chats we were having over drinks after the tennis session.

Case Study: Eric Vatikiotis-Bateson

(Professor of Linguistics and Director of Cognitive Systems Program at University of British Columbia)

Professor Vatikiotis-Bateson and his family moved from the United States to Japan in 1990. He had previously experienced Japanese culture during two short stays. He joined the Advanced Telecommunications Research Institute International (ATR) as Invited Researcher with plans to stay for two years.

Since learning to speak Japanese competently is extremely difficult, he decided it would be a more efficient use of his limited time to focus entirely on his research.

However, he and his family ended up living in Japan for thirteen years.

Not speaking the language was not a problem with his Japanese colleagues. This enabled them to have a relationship with him sufficiently distant to feel comfortable. It even became an advantage for Eric. It allowed him to avoid conforming to the Japanese ways of doing things and their approval processes. He also became a conduit for Japanese colleagues who discovered that many things could be done more directly and faster via English.

After some years in Japan, he discerned a system of recognition that was very different in Japan than in his home country. For instance, recognition for good work was not explicit. In the USA he would have received, at least, a 'pat on the back'. Instead, in Japan, his project's budget was increased regularly.

> Despite the advantages of not speaking the language, if he were to start again, Professor Vatikiotis-Bateson says he would begin his stay in Japan with an intensive, six-month course in Japanese language. His aim would not be to use Japanese as the workplace transaction language. It would be to overhear things, listen-in better, and avoid cultural misunderstandings.
>
> Eric's advice: 'You can do your job anywhere in the world. However, that doesn't mean you can *live* anywhere in the world.'

Prepare to build trust step by step

Expect your networking activities to take more time than in your home country.

Due to multiple factors, building a good network of contacts in your new country will take longer than you expect and, of course, longer than in your home country.

You have just arrived in your new country and would like to have a big network of local contacts really soon. You might be tempted to cast a wide net to increase your odds. You could start phoning people listed in your trade association's membership with the objective of scheduling lots of appointments. Don't be fooled into doing so.

Take your time to fine tune your self-introduction (see chapter *Your self-introduction: a memorable single sentence*). Your first meeting should not be with the top people on your potential list of contacts. You want to approach them once you have a well-tuned self-introduction to the culture and manners of your new country. You will be more confident in delivering it after you have practised in real situations several times.

Before making contact, you need to assess how you can help every one of them. It would be impossible to do it by phoning a full membership list. So, take your time to investigate the potential value you can bring to each of them. For instance, let's imagine you have a list of one hundred names and phone numbers in your trade association. You can quickly select those you can help. This will take about five seconds per name (a total of 500 seconds or just above eight minutes). Suppose you have twenty names remaining.

You then do a second pass where you investigate more deeply into how you can help each person. You can do this by using online tools such as LinkedIn, Google, and their personal or corporate web pages. It might be worth keeping the information in a common place. I normally do this with a plain spreadsheet for easy access. This will take about five minutes per person (a total of one hour and forty minutes).

You can establish the order in which you want to approach them. This might take a total of five minutes. You will plan first to meet a handful of people who will not be your top targets (because of their status or visibility). These first meetings will allow you to practise and fine tune the way you present yourself. It will also allow you to adapt your speech and manners to the local culture. Once you feel you are ready, you can approach the rest of your short list, which in our example was of twenty people.

Your preparation has taken just under two hours. It has been an investment to get maximum benefit from the meetings you will have in the following weeks.

NETWORKING ACROSS A NEW COUNTRY / 89

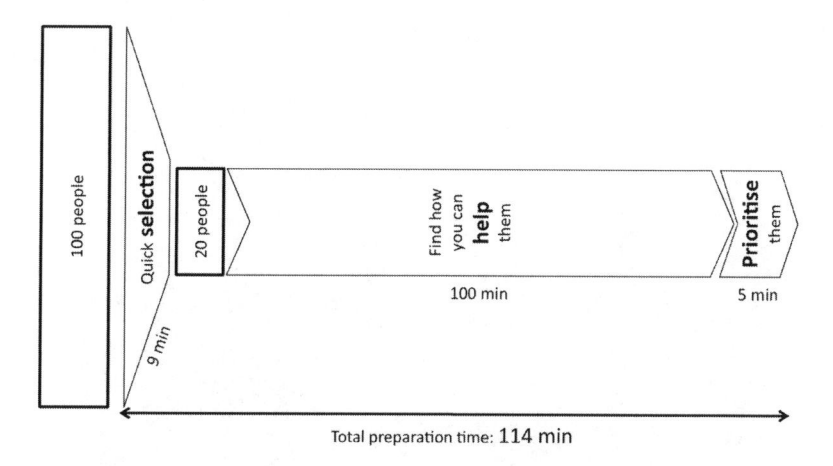

Investment in meeting preparation.

When you start meeting people, take your time to build trust. Some people might not give you names and information easily at the first meeting. This does not mean they do not want to share information with you. It just means that you need to take your time to build trust with them. The trust-building pace changes considerably from culture to culture and from person to person. As usual, you should listen between the lines during your meetings to estimate ways you can give value to that person. Then do whatever you need to do to help that person until you meet them again. The help can come in many ways. If none comes to your mind, you can revert to the old and well-tested method of praising your counterpart. You can read his or her book or article in the press and send a quick note expressing your admiration and reasons for liking it. Top people need praise too! Some feel very lonely[9] and spend most of their time fighting internal (or external) politics. Receiving a positive note always helps.

---

9 See for instance 'It's not just lonely at the top; it can be disengaging, too' article in USA Today (6th June 2005): http://www.usatoday.com/money/companies/management/2005-06-20-bummed-execs_x.htm (accessed on 10th November 2010).

Building

Connect with diverse people. Organise dinners. Join relevant clubs.

Visit your new country

Visit your new country before you move there.

If you haven't moved into your new (or target) country yet, schedule a visit.

If you are building your network in advance as part of your efforts to get a job there or even start a company, you should visit the new country as often as possible. The face-to-face meetings will be strategic building blocks in your network. How often should that be? It will depend on the difficulty and cost of travel. For instance, if your move is between two European capitals, you should go as often as you can and, if possible, during weekdays. The more often you go, the faster and stronger your network will grow. On the other hand, if your move is intercontinental you cannot expect to go every month. Try to go as often as you can. For instance, before we moved back to Europe from Australia, I tried to be in Europe at least once every ten months.

In some cases you might manage to go every six months and in others every two years. Whatever the frequency, it should be the best you can achieve.

When visiting your target country you will have several advantages over the local networkers. People will make time to meet you because:

- You are coming from abroad. The further away you are coming from, the more likely it will be that people will make time for you.
- People want to know about your country. The more exotic your country is (in their minds), the better.

Before the trip

Ensure you prepare for your trip. You should try to schedule meetings for at least your first two days there. You might be a great networker and you know that it is advisable to use the phone when requesting meetings (see chapter *To speak or to write?*). However, due to the distance, and maybe time difference, you will be tempted to use email. It might work in some cases. However, you do not know in advance which cases those are. My recommendation is to use the phone and follow up by email. If you speak to a personal assistant (or gatekeeper) remember to use his or her name when you follow up in a few days' time. Most probably you will have to phone back and you want to make sure the gate is open.

Let's imagine that you have scheduled a meeting with a relevant person in the manufacturing industry in your new country. Today you happen to read an article relating to the evolution of manufacturing during the last fifty years. To lay the groundwork before your meeting, you could send the article to that person. However, do not rush to the photocopier. Rush to the newsstand! You do not want to send a black and white photocopy of such a wonderfully produced article. You want to send the original. So instead, you:

- Buy another copy of the magazine,
- Put a post-it note on the relevant page,
- Write a cover letter, and
- Mail it all together.

The most important preparation before the trip is finding ways to help the people you will be meeting. What are the main challenges each of them is facing? Gather as much information as you can and brainstorm ideas that can be of value to them. Is there something you can bring from your country that would be of help? Can any of your previous experiences be relevant to them? You need to think about these and other questions. There is no single solution that fits all. You need to spend time thinking about each individual you will be meeting.

During the trip

The meetings you had scheduled before departing will be the starting point of your construction efforts. Some of the people you will meet might not be relevant to your network. Some others will be excellent contacts. No matter what category the person you are meeting falls into, you should always ask for recommendations of other people to meet.

It might even happen that the person you are speaking to volunteers to make an introduction to someone else. This is one of those situations where your advantage over the local networkers comes into play. The person might phone a colleague and say something like, 'Joe from Uruguay is just visiting for two days. Do you have some time tomorrow to meet him? In fact he hoped you might allow him to invite you out for lunch.'

Your visit to the country will allow you to gather information about your sector. Buy as many trade journals as you can. Some journals and magazines are only partially accessible via the Internet. You should also wander around the districts where the relevant companies are located. This will allow you to get a feel for the differences between your home country and the new one. You might have a serendipitous encounter with a relevant individual. However, do not count on it and do not push for it.

After the trip

Obviously, when you return to your home country you should follow up every contact you have made. A letter is a great way to do this. If possible use real stamps on your letter, not the postage meter imprint. Stamps help your letter (and you) to stand out from the rest. For instance, when I sent letters from Australia to Europe, prior to our moving there, I always ensured that the stamp depicted a koala or a kangaroo.

And then start preparing for your *next* visit to that country!

Connect via your weak ties

People neither close nor similar to you will provide very useful contacts in your network.

Your weakest ties are the people who will give you the most contacts in your new country (see chapter *Weak ties are stronger*). Let me give you an example.

Let's suppose that in four months Joanne starts a three-year-long assignment to the Ivory Coast. She wants to start building her network before she gets there but she doesn't know where to begin. Last year, during an executive education course, she met Pierre. They had a brief conversation during which Pierre mentioned he was born to French parents on the Ivory Coast. When he was twenty years old, he had stayed behind when his parents returned to France. Since then he has continued to work on the Ivory Coast for the same company, which operates in a completely different sector from Joanne's.

At the time of their conversation this was not particularly interesting to Joanne. However, now it was a different story. She saw him as her golden opportunity to start building her Ivory Coast network. She contacted him. After a few emails and one phone call they agreed to meet during her first week on the Ivory Coast. Six months later, when Joanne looks at her local contacts, she can trace 80% of them to either Pierre or one of his contacts.

From the previous example, you will appreciate that if you can find someone in your network who is based in your new country, or who has strong connections there, you should not underestimate his or her value. Do not be biased by your contact's job title or rank.

Online tools, such as LinkedIn, will show who, within your network, has contacts in your new country. You can easily search for contacts. Such online sites offer tools to contact directly those friends of your friends. *Don't do it!* This is pretty close to sending emails to a list of addresses gathered from the yellow pages. Yes, you can read spam emails if you wish. It is pretty much what you would be doing.

A much better approach would be the following:

- Identify individuals in your target country.
- Sort them by relationship connection.
- Keep only the direct contacts or second connection ones (which

means that there is only one individual between you and them).
- For the direct contacts, contact them, of course.
- For the rest, you should approach personally (by email or phone) each connecting individual (someone who is between you and them) to seek an introduction.

You ask them if they could make an introduction to their contact in that country. You will find that in some cases they do not really know each other and thus the introduction will not be very effective, if it ever happens at all. In some other cases, the connecting individual will introduce you to the other person, most probably by sending an email to both of you. An alternative, even if not as desirable, is for you to ask the connecting individuals if you can use their name when contacting the other person.

You might be thinking that this is too labour-intensive. Online tools were supposed to make your life easier, weren't they? In a sense you are right. However, you are trying to create trust relationships. They take time. In addition, you need to stand out from the crowd of individuals using automated requests. Remember, as mentioned above, it is not the *quantity* of connections that counts but their *quality*.

Do not restrict yourself to online tools. Liz Lynch, author of *Smart Networking*, warns us to 'Keep in mind that online networks enable relationships, not take the place of them.' You should also search your memory for ideas on potential acquaintances with connections in your future country. For instance, let's suppose that Andrew has just arrived in Chile because his wife is opening a local subsidiary there. Before leaving his previous country, Andrew couldn't find anyone from Chile on his LinkedIn network.

Once in Chile, by chance he walked in front of a high school in

Santiago de Chile and had a flashback. He remembered that a Chilean girl, Martina, had attended his high school. At the time, he knew her but they were not friends. He never saw her again and heard that she had returned to Chile. A quick Google search allowed him to locate Martina. She was extremely happy to reconnect with Andrew. She provided him with very useful introductions. One year later, Andrew started a services company and his first employee was Martina!

A research report by *Accenture* and the University of Virginia summarises it as 'Top performers understand the value of networks and engage in behaviours that lead to high-quality relationships — not just big networks.' Forget about meeting people for the sake of meeting people. Meet people to move towards your objective. Of course, this does not mean that you should decline invitations to events or to meet people. As Hugh Gyton recommends (see his case study below), 'Do not decline invitations to meet new people.' However, you need to follow up with the people who will help achieve your objective. You need to avoid spending too much effort on the rest. Remember that there are only twenty-four hours in a day and you need to get some sleep!

If we take our road-building analogy, never turn down a surveying opportunity. This will help you map the territory. You will be more selective when you decide where to build the roads. In other words, you will select who you want to engage in a deeper relationship. When you decide to foster one relationship, always look for opportunities to provide value to that relationship.

Sometimes it seems difficult to find ways to offer something that the other person will find helpful. Your mind keeps drifting towards how the other person will help *you*. If you are stuck in such a situation one mental trick might help unblock your thinking. Close your eyes; take two deep breaths and imagine that they have offered you excellent advice (or whatever else you think that person can give you). That's it! You've got it! He or she has given you as much as they can. So now your mind can stop thinking about the benefits you will receive. Instead you can imagine the other person in their work. You might get some insight into what help you could provide. If it does not happen immediately, keep imagining that person in their personal life. Does he or she practice a sport? Or does he like travelling? What else? Probably you will discover new ideas that can be of value. If that is not the case, you should repeat the exercise later in the day. More probably than not you will get great ideas that will help the other person.

Case Study: Hugh Gyton

(Principal, Conversations Matter)

Hugh Gyton moved from the UK to Australia in 1985 to establish the Australian subsidiary for his employer, Comshare Ltd.

While waiting for his immigration visa, Hugh compiled a list of twenty people in Sydney, mainly friends of friends.

On arrival in Australia he contacted everyone on his list in a very disciplined and methodical way. He met each of them at least once. He never declined any offer to participate in an activity that could bring new contacts.

Those efforts provided the foundation for his extensive and useful network in his new country.

> Hugh's advice: 'Your attitude is key. Go with an open mind and embrace every opportunity, even if it is something that you would not normally do in your home country.'

Interview executives

Interviewing executives for an article in a trade magazine will give you an excellent reason to meet the most unapproachable people.

In chapter *Write articles in trade magazines* you read about the usefulness of writing articles to gain visibility. It will prove most useful in your network creation efforts in a new country.

However, your main objective now is not the article or its publication. It is conducting interviews with local executives. Writing an article is the means to get such interviews. Keith Ferrazzi writes in his book *Never Eat Alone*, 'You can get close to almost anyone by doing a piece on them, or with them, even if it's for your local newspaper.'

At the end of the day, it is not very important which trade magazine your write for as long as it allows you to interview the relevant people. You do not need to approach the top trade magazine. However, the better known the magazine is, the easier it will be for you to get interviews. It might be better to have a small piece in a renowned magazine than a very long article in a lesser known one. View the article as a 'door opener'. The former, even if smaller, will open more doors than the latter.

How do you get an article commissioned by a top trade magazine? Most magazines are always on the lookout for fresh content. You should use this to your advantage. You are new to the country and thus you can provide a new perspective on an old problem. If you have difficulty with this approach, why not do it the other way around? You can write the article and then submit it for consideration to the magazine. When approaching potential interviewees you do not need to tell them whether the article has been commissioned or if it will be submitted for consideration at a later date. You just say, 'Your views would greatly add to the value of the article I am currently writing for the XYZ Magazine.'

What if you don't feel comfortable writing for a trade magazine in your new country? Do you have problems writing long pieces in the local language? Then you can write for a magazine in your home country. Their readers will be interested to know about their industry in your new country. Some of the potential interviewees might even feel more comfortable with an interview published abroad.

You might feel tempted to use an article in your blog to secure the interviews. This should be your very last option. Publishing a blog is so easy that it provides no extra benefit to the interviewee. Of course, this does not apply if your blog is the top blog in your industry or enjoys a readership of hundreds of thousands.

Overall you will use the interviews to:

- Gather information on the interviewee's challenges and the potential areas where you could provide valuable input.
- Gain visibility with the interviewee by stating your well-rehearsed self-introduction. (The self-introduction is a memorable single sentence that you use when introducing yourself to people for the first time; see chapter *Your self-introduction: a memorable single sentence*).
- Learn about the country and your particular industry in that country.
- And, of course, get some content for your article.

During the interview you can, as usual, ask them to recommend other people you might contact. After the interview, you should send a thank-you note. If at any time in the future, even the distant future, you come across information that might help solve his or her issues, you should pass it on without delay.

Ensure that you send a copy of the published article to everyone you have interviewed. You wanted the interviews more than the article itself so you might forget about it as soon as you send the final version of your text to the magazine. Make a note in your diary (or wherever you note things you must remember) about sending copies of the article. This will be a great opportunity to foster a deeper relationship with the interviewees.

While the article is current, you can use it as a further door opener. Depending on the publication, an article is seen as current for six months to a year. During this time, you can send the article to someone you want to contact. It will give you some credibility that you would not otherwise have.

Help in trade missions

Being involved in trade missions between your home country and your new one will prove a source of valuable contacts.

Why not help to organise a trade mission between your home country and your new country? You will leverage your previous contacts.

Perhaps a local chamber of commerce, or similar body, is already organising such a mission. In that case, you should volunteer to help the chamber of commerce. You should detail your expertise and previous contacts. This will ensure that you are given tasks that will allow you to meet people. You don't want to spend all of your time folding letters and stuffing envelopes!

If the two countries do not share the same language and you happen to speak both, you will be in a great position to meet lots of interesting new people. Ensure that you are not perceived as a translator or interpreter. You want to be seen as a top professional who happens to have very good language skills. Thus, when you meet for the first time you can deliver your self-introduction (see chapter *Your self-introduction: a memorable single sentence*). If you exchange business cards it will become obvious what your professional area is.

If there is no local chamber of commerce that has such plans, try finding a chamber of commerce (or similar association such as the Rotary Club) in your home country that might be interested in your new country. They will love to have a trusted person at the other end. You will be their local voice. They will be your door opener into great new contacts.

Think wider about trade missions. For instance, big events are potential equivalents to trade missions. Three times I have happened to live in (or very close to) the city that hosted the Olympic Games. They attract many business people and government officials. You will be the trusted person on the ground for the people visiting from your home country. Be pro-active. Let them know that you are there. You could even set up some activity or city tour.

Unfortunately, at the time I was too busy in my job and frankly such opportunities didn't even occur to me. Thus I ended up being reactive to the visitors. Despite the lack of 'pro-activeness', excellent networking opportunities came my way. One even led to a job offer!

Virtual trade missions are now possible too. They entail two groups of people, one in each country. One group is in a teleconference room in one country, while the other is in a similar room in the other country. People can have productive exchanges despite the physical distance. Being able to see the other faces helps build trust. However, when you organise or participate in a virtual trade mission between your home country and your new one, your main objective is to connect with the people who are in the same room as you (in your new country).

The virtual trade mission enables you to meet people in your new country. You will have great opportunities to contact people during the preparation of the virtual trade mission. With some of them you will start to build trust before the meeting, during the meeting and after the meeting. You will have many opportunities for informal chats outside the formal meeting. Each of these opportunities will be a chance to use your self-introduction and gather information on how you can help executives in your new country.

Join the right clubs

When choosing which clubs to join, focus on your objective, not just your comfort.

Clubs and associations are frameworks that allow connections to be made. Put yourself into the most relevant frameworks!

A golden rule before joining a club is to attend at least two of their events. Some clubs might look very good on paper but be very different in reality. For instance, a poetry writers' association I almost joined while living in France turned out to be just a monthly dinner where a handful of wannabe poets read their long poems and expected applause at the end. When you attend an event, you will get to know members and see what type of activities they are involved in.

Despite your willingness to network, the day has only twenty-four hours and the week only seven days. Thus you need to pick your battles. You cannot join every club and association you might wish to join. You need to be active in the ones you join and not just be an attendee at events (see *Become involved association* on page 62).

Expat clubs, a potential trap

Which clubs to join? The first one that comes to mind is the expats club formed by people from your home country. You will be able to speak your own language and get tips from people who have made the same transition before you. Beware, though you may be joining it for your own comfort. Do not see it as one of your big networking opportunities. More often than not, people who join expat clubs end up trapped in old-country contacts and mindsets. It is one of the examples where your network can be a liability and hold you back from making relevant contacts. You may end up getting local contacts through members of the expat club. However, in most cases it may not be the most effective way of getting those contacts. The following is one example of what might happen if you focus only on your expat club.

One year after we moved to Sydney, we met two Spaniards who had just started a three-year job in Sydney with the organisation of the Olympic Games 2000. One of them, let's call him Andrés, joined the 'Casa de España'. The other, let's call him Pepe, joined the 'Surry Hills Chess Club'. During his first six months, Pepe had a hard time breaking into the local group. The opposite happened to Andrés, who had a very easy time and he could even eat familiar Spanish food.

After that initial period however, their fortunes changed. Pepe developed a thriving social life and even had job offers. On the other hand, Andrés started thinking that the effort he had put into moving to Sydney might have been useless. He might just as well have been back in Spain!

David McLellan gives a similar perspective in his case study (see page 63). However, expat clubs could be your only way forward when foreigners form the bulk of a country's population (e.g., United Arab Emirates) or the culture is remarkably different from yours (e.g., Hong Kong). Such is the case of Sally Foley-Lewis (see below).

If we forget about the expat clubs, what clubs are left? There are basically two types:

- Professional associations or clubs in your field, and
- Leisure clubs.

Professional associations or clubs

Joining a professional association or club will allow you to connect with people like yourself. You'll be able to discuss work issues and solve common problems. But if you are working in a corporation, most probably you will meet similar people during your everyday activities. Thus you can concentrate your efforts on the leisure clubs (see below). However, if you work for a small company or if you are working alone, professional associations can bring you excellent benefits.

In some countries it's easy to locate a relevant professional association or club. This is often the case in Anglo-Saxon countries where they tend to be formalised and publicised. In other countries, they may be a kind of informal arrangement. This could be the case in southern European countries. You will need to make an extra effort to locate appropriate groups. For instance, you might want to read local newspapers to identify relevant advertisements.

When you talk to people during your networking efforts, do not hesitate to ask which association or club they would recommend you to join. It will be a great way, on the one hand, to discover groups that you would not know about and, on the other hand, to nurture the relationship with the person who made the recommendation.

Leisure clubs

Joining a leisure club will provide you with lots of weak ties (for the importance of weak ties see chapter *Weak ties are stronger*). However, you should put some thought into which leisure club to join. Among other things, consider:

- A leisure activity you are passionate about. Otherwise, the effort needed to attend events will be too high.
- The current club membership. The members should be in your target market. You will get more out of your membership if the affiliates are professionals, managers or executives, whether active or retired.
- The location of the activities. You should look at two aspects. One is the convenience relative to your home location. The other is the proximity to a suburb where your target market lives.
- Participation in activities with something at stake. If the activities are in the public eye, you will be more likely to develop trust with the other members. This is called the 'shared activities principle' (see chapter *Develop trust through informal shared activities*).

Whatever clubs you join, be they professional or leisure, make sure your membership benefits them. Do not miss any opportunity, be it in assisting in organizing the annual dinner or making phone calls about upcoming events. When you feel you can really assist the executive committee, do not hesitate to volunteer for it. This is exactly what David McLellan has done every time he has moved to a new country (see his case study on page 63).

> ### Case Study: Sally Foley-Lewis
>
> (Trainer, speaker, coach)
>
> Sally and her husband moved to Abu Dhabi (United Arab Emirates) in 2005 where they then spent five years.
>
> While waiting for the visa procedure to be completed, she did background research on the country. She read relevant books such as *Culture Shock U.A.E.* and *SBS World Guide*. A few months beforehand, her brother-in-law had moved to the Emirates. He provided her with good advice too. Once they arrived in Abu Dhabi their moving company offered them the book *Abu Dhabi Explorer*, which was full of great advice for expats.
>
> Foreigners make up a large part of the population of the Emirates (approximately 85%). Sally says, 'In the Emirates you stick to your own culture. Your social network stays within it. Your business network is larger and goes beyond your culture.'
>
> She joined several clubs at different times during her stay in the Emirates. All the jobs she had came via the network in one club or another. For instance, her job as trade consultant with the Australian Trade Commission came via a person she met at the

> British Club. Another example is her position as senior management consultant for a local training company, which she got via her contacts at the International Business Women's Group Abu Dhabi.
>
> Sally's advice:
>
> - Hunt out a good range of resources. Read them and don't take them at face value!
> - Take your time to get to know and understand the cultures that are in your target country. Be wary of your own assumptions!
> - Seek contacts in the target country. Ask their advice. Social media websites can help you in your discovery efforts.

Dinner at home

Organising themed dinners will convert contacts into networking links.

You can organise dinners at home. Invite people you want to get to know better and with whom you want to develop links. In some cultures inviting people for dinner at home might be a very strange thing to do and even have negative connotations. You will find this out during your cultural investigations (see chapter *Explore the country's culture*). If this is the case, feel free to skip this chapter. But before skipping it, think about adapting the tip. You can investigate potential alternatives, such as dining at a restaurant or at a cultural venue.

In many cultures, people feel honoured when someone invites them to their home. This chapter provides some ideas that my family and I have put into practice, sometimes when starting a period in a foreign country and other times when returning to our home country.

You organise a dinner at your place to which you invite people. They do not need to know each other. In fact, if everyone knows each other it is more a friends' dinner than a networking dinner. It can even be a good way to introduce two people to each other. If this is the case, in addition to constructing your network, you will also be maintaining it. You will be providing considerable benefits to the people you are introducing.

Have a theme or topic

It is important to have a theme or topic for the event. Since most people do not know each other, having a theme can ease the conversation, in particular at the beginning of the dinner. The following are potential themes that I have either used or seen someone else using:

- Photos and places. Every attendee brings a photo. The photos are put together and shown in random order. Everyone has to guess who brought the photo and where it was taken.
- Foods. Everyone has to bring a dish of a specific colour, for instance yellow. Variations include period topics (such as 1960s food), geographical topics (Asian or Mexican food), and nostalgia topics (a preferred dish from your childhood).
- Quotes. Everyone brings a quote that encompasses his/her feelings about last year. The quotes are read aloud and everyone else needs to guess why he or she chose it. Variations include newspaper articles and book titles.

Do not expect that everyone will discuss your chosen theme throughout the evening. Remember that you chose a theme to help start the conversation among people who do not know each other. It may happen that, sooner than you expect, a lively conversation springs up about other matters. In other cases, your guests may not feel at ease with each other. They can then stick to the chosen topic. It will allow pleasant interaction to continue during the whole meal.

Whom to invite

When you think about whom to invite, consider two more names than the number you expect to attend. Dinners with between six and twelve people generate lively interaction and discussion. With less than six people, the dinner can end up being a boring meal. With more than twelve, it can become a noisy event where not everyone gets to talk to each other. It can be good fun but it will not be the type of networking event you aimed for.

When you send out the invitations it is advisable to ask for any dietary restrictions. You should also let everyone know who else has been invited. It gives your guests a chance to prepare in advance, and may avoid spending several hours in your home with two people who don't speak to each other. It happened to me once, and I promise that I will not let it happen again!

Obviously, you should invite spouses too. Keep in mind that you can get more interaction between people if spouses do not sit next to each other. You might want to put name cards in each place, thus staying in control of who sits where. I prefer not to do this as it becomes too formal and so does the dinner.

My apartment is too small...

Do not be discouraged if you would like to have themed dinners but think that your place is too small. You can get good advice in the book *Never Eat Alone*. For instance, you can:

- Invite fewer people.
- Have a cocktail party instead of a sit-down dinner.
- Use a friend's place.
- Hold a picnic in a public park.
- Rent a function room.

Whatever you decide to do, you need to be comfortable with it. If you are proud of yourself and your dinner, everyone else will be happy too. If you do not feel at ease, this feeling will spread to your guests like a virus. Be a great host in your preferred setting!

Case Study: Martha Mollison

(Director, Dancing Iris Video Pty. Ltd.)

Martha Mollison took the 'dinner at home' technique to the next level. She used it to survey the new territory and contact potential links for her network.

When Martha Mollison moved from the USA to Australia in 1986 she had no contacts within the video industry. She organised the première screening of her latest documentary at a dinner in her apartment.

Martha attended a local conference. From the contacts made at the conference, she compiled a list of ten women involved in video media around Sydney. She invited them to the première. About five of them attended the event.

That dinner in her small apartment provided Martha with many benefits:

- She established trusted connections.
- She established visibility amongst video industry players.
- She even received a job offer!

One of the people who could not attend the event phoned to apologise. During the phone conversation the caller mentioned, 'By the way, you should contact X from the Australian Film, Television and Radio School because he wants to hire someone.' Martha followed up with X who shortly afterwards offered her a job.

Since that time Martha has had multiple teaching appointments and has published many editions of her Australian bestseller *Producing Videos: A Complete Guide*.

Maintaining

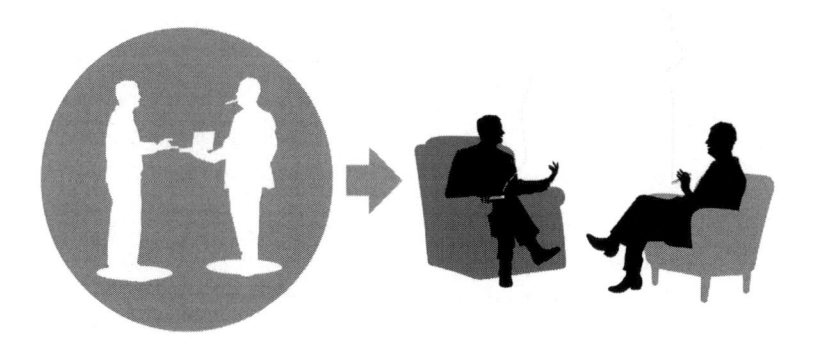

Benefit from your trips back home. Keep your network informed.

Visit back home

Your trips back to your previous country will provide many opportunities to deliver value to your network.

Make the most of your trips back home.

If you have already moved to your new country, most probably you will go back home every now and then.[10] Take advantage of such trips to nurture the contacts in your new country.

Depending on your home country it might be very easy to see how you can help your new contacts. The help can come in many ways and forms. You can put in contact people from both countries. This would be similar to developing bridges between industries or professions (see chapter *Develop bridges with your previous industries*). You need to think further than giving sales referrals from one country to the other.

You can also provide non-work value to your contacts. A straightforward example comes from a Cuban. Every time he went back to Cuba, he returned to his new country with cigars for the people he knew were cigar lovers. Another example comes from my own experience. While living in Australia, when I visited my home country Andorra I used to buy stamps, which are appreciated by anyone who has a stamp collection, even if it is a simple one.

While you are visiting your home country, keep in the back of your mind the potential help to your contacts. For instance, you might read

---

10 You will find very useful advice on 'The Art of Coming Home', C. Storti (2001), Intercultural Press

an article in the local newspaper that might be of interest to some of your new contacts. Depending on your current relationship with that person you can choose one of two options.

If you are well acquainted with your contact, you can send the article to them straight away. You send it by post with a nice stamp, so you stand out from the crowd. In addition, if you have it in electronic format, you can send it via email. This will allow your contact to reply easily. You can have a brief email conversation and see if there are other things you can do while you are in your home country that can be of help to your contact.

The other option, if you are in the early stages of a relationship with that contact, is that you can keep the article to give it to him or her on your return. Keep a note with the article to remind you whom you intend to give it to and the main reason why you thought about them. This will be a good reason to meet him or her again and strengthen your relationship.

Keep reporting back

Have strategies to make sure that you report back about your progress to the relevant people in your network.

Building your network in a new country takes a long time. Thus it becomes very important to keep reporting back to your new contacts and letting them know about your progress.

The well-known saying applies: 'Out of sight, out of mind'. If you are not in touch regularly with your new contacts you will not be in their minds. Since your networking efforts will be slow, it is very easy to forget to update them about your progress. The following is an example of what might happen unless you are proactive about it.

Let's suppose that Keith has just arrived to Brazil. He meets Kate, who is the editor in chief of a local trade magazine. Kate suggests that he should contact Joao, the president of the Brazilian Manufacturing Association. Keith's efforts to meet Joao do not bring immediate results. He keeps contacting Joao; soon even Joao's personal assistant knows Keith's voice when he phones. After six months of trying, Joao agrees to talk to Keith during the coffee break at a national conference.

Six months is a long time, so Keith forgets about updating Kate and letting her know about his meeting with Joao. When two days later Joao meets Kate at their bi-monthly industry gathering, she learns about the meeting of Joao and Keith. On one hand, she is glad it worked out well for Keith. On the other hand, she feels somehow let down by Keith, as she would have liked to have known about it from Keith.

Keith could have followed two strategies to avoid this:

1. He could have updated Kate every couple of months on how he was getting on. Of course, he would not have put it in a negative way, such as 'Joao does not want to meet me.' He would use a positive view, such as 'Joao's personal assistant is being very helpful. Joao and I should be able to meet in the future.' These updates to Kate would have reminded her about the advice she gave Keith. Probably she would even have mentioned it to Joao at one of the bi-monthly gatherings.

2. He could have a method to keep track of whom he has already thanked and whom he still needs to thank. This can be done with a spreadsheet with one column for the advisers' names, another for

the referrals and a third column where he puts a cross once he has updated the adviser about his contact with the referral. If Keith prefers having this information with his electronic address book, he can do it using user-defined fields. They could be named 'advised by', and 'adviser updated after meeting'.

One way you can stay in people's minds is by reporting about your progress on contacting the referrals they recommended. This will break the cycle of being out of sight, which makes you out of mind, which in turn makes harder for you to progress in your networking efforts.

Practice and Adapt Your Learning

Practice the tips, one by one

In the introduction you read that you need to get out and apply your reading so that it becomes learning. Now you are about to finish reading. You will need to start applying.

Do not try doing too much to start with. It is much better to advance with small steps than to try doing big steps but not completing them. Networking in a new environment is effort intensive as you will be out of your comfort zone.

Choose one, and only one, thing from the book to put into practice. You should select the tip that you feel most comfortable with instead of the one that you imagine will bring the best results. This will enable you to get your feet wet before going for a proper swim.

Once you have practiced the selected tip a few times and you feel comfortable with it, go and select another one. This way you will keep increasing your networking toolbox and avoid the overwhelming feeling of trying too many new things at once.

Adapt the tips

Networking techniques and tools need to be adapted to your way of doing things and not the other way around.

You might not feel really comfortable about one of the tips in this book. However, you know it would be very beneficial to you and your network. Thus, adapt the tip so that it can be executed to suit you.

The following is an extreme example. Let's suppose that you cannot use the phone because you have hearing difficulties. You can interact face-to-face. However, when speaking over the phone, your interlocutor needs to repeat one sentence every now and again. You can adapt the tips in the book that relate to phone conversation to another communication medium. Keep in mind the essence of the tip. For instance, I have recommended using the phone primarily because the phone allows real time responses and reactions. You should try to find a medium with these characteristics that gets as close as possible to the phone. In some cases, you might be able to message via Twitter. In some other cases, you might try a face-to-face 'serendipitous' encounter.

Adapt this book to suit your personal style while keeping the spirit of the tips.

Further Reading and References

Books

P. Bethencourt (2008): *El éxito en seis cafés*, Gestion 2000.

H. Bommelaer (2008): *Booster sa carrière grâce au Réseau*, Éditions Eyrolles.

B. Brough et al. (2007): *Strategic Networking - Your Guide to Networking Excellence*, Sea Change Publishing.

R. Burt (2009): Network Duality of Social Capital, chapter in *Social Capital: Reaching Out, Reaching In*, ed. V.O. Bartkus & J.H. Davis. (Edward Elgar).

D. Darling (2003): *The Networking Survival Guide*, McGraw-Hill.

K. Ferrazzi & T. Raz (2005): *Never Eat Alone: And Other Secrets to Success, One Relationship at a Time*, Crown Business.

L. Lynch (2008): *Smart Networking: Attract a Following In Person and Online*, McGraw-Hill.

I. Misner, D. Alexander & B. Hilliard (2009): *Networking Like a Pro: Turning contacts into connections*, Entrepreneur Press.

D. Rayback (2010): *ConnectAbility*, McGraw Hill.

S. RoAne (2007): *How to Work a Room*, Harper Paperbacks.

B. Tomalin & M. Nicks (2010): *The World's business cultures and how to unlock them*, Thorogood Publishing (2010).

J. Vermeiren (2007): *Let's Connect*, Morgan James Publishing.

J. Vermeiren (2009): *How to REALLY use LinkedIn*, BookSurge Publishing.

Other references

R. Burt (1997): Maximize Your Social Capital, A New Guide to Networking, *Capital Ideals*, Vol. 1, No. 1.

R. Burt (1998): Personality Correlates of Structural Holes; *Social Networks*, 20(1).

R. Burt, R.M. Hogarth & C. Michaud (2000): The Social Capital of French and American Managers, *Organization Science*, 11(2).

W.C. Byham (2009): Start Networking Right Away (Even If You Hate It), *Harvard Business Review*, January 2009.

G. Corkindale (2009): 6 Networking Mistakes And How to Avoid Them, *Harvard Business Publishing Blogs*. Accessed on 19th November 2009 at: http://blogs.harvardbusiness.org/corkindale/2009/04/6_networking _mistakes_and_how.html

R. Cross, R.J. Thomas & D.A. Light (2006): *How Top Talent Uses Networks and Where Rising Stars Get Trapped*, Research Report Accenture. Accessed on 12 August 2010 at: www.robcross.org/pdf/roundtable/high_performer_networks_and_traps.pdf

R. Cross, T.H. Davenport & S. Cantrell (2003): The Social Side of Performance, *MIT Sloan Management Review*, Volume 45, Number 1, pages 20–22.

K. Ferrazzi (2009): *15 Tips from Keith Ferrazzi, Conference Commando!*, Ferrazzi Greenlight.

M. Gargiulo & M. Benassi (2000): Trapped in Your Own Net? Network Cohesion, Structural Holes, and the Adaptation of Social Capital, *Organization Science*, 11(2).

M.S. Granovetter (1973): The Strength of Weak Ties, *The American Journal of Sociology*, Vol 78. No. 6 (May 1973), pages 1360–1380. Available at http://smg.media.mit.edu/classes/library/granovetter.weak.ties/granovetter.htm

H. Ibarra (2008): Networking is vital for successful managers, *Insead Knowledge*: http://knowledge.insead.edu/contents/Ibarra.cfm (accessed on 28th January 2010).

H. Ibarra & M. Hunter (2007) How Leaders Create and Use Networks. *Harvard Business Review*, January 2007.

M. Javidan, M. Teagarden, & David Bowen (2010): Managing Yourself: Making It Overseas, *Harvard Business Review* 88(4), April 2010.

G. Matthews (2007): *Goals Research Summary*, http://www.dominican.edu/academics/ahss/psych/faculty/fulltime/gailmatthews/researchsummary2.pdf (accessed 9th November 2010).

I. Maurer & M. Ebers (2006): Dynamics of Social Capital and their Performance Implications: Lessons from Biotechnology Start-ups; *Administrative Science Quarterly*, vol. 51, Issue 2, pages 262-292.

B. Uzzi & S. Dunlap (2005): How to Build Your Network, *Harvard Business Review*, December 2005, 83(12): pages 53-60.

J. Vermeiren (2007): *Let's Connect (Free Light version)*, available at http://www.letsconnect.be/light-version.html

J. Vermeiren (2008): *Listening*, www.networking-coach.com/en-luisteren.html, accessed on December 17th 2009.

J. Vermeiren (2009): *How to REALLY use LinkedIn (Free Light version)*, available at http://www.how-to-really-use-linkedin.com/en-lightversion.html

P. Wagner & L. Smith (1980): *The Networking Game*, booklet accessed on 2nd December 2009 at www.pattern.com/game1980.html

Acknowledgements

I would like to thank everyone who has helped in some shape or form during the making of this book. In particular, for their comments on the draft text, my gratitude goes to John Pinnell, Albert Mora i Gonzàlez, Jaume Benavent i Guàrdia and Xavier Maymó i Gatell; and for support with language issues to Clare Allcard and Judith Wood.

I specially want to thank the people who shared their experiences in the case studies: Amy Jenner, Catherine DeVrye, Chris Golis, David McLellan, Eric Vatikiotis-Bateson, Gary Linnane, Hugh Gyton, J Patrick (JP) Bewley, Martha Mollison, Martin Varsavsky and Sally Foley-Lewis.

I ought to emphasise the unconditional patience of my family: Núria, Ïa and Ester.

Connecting Forward is also available in Spanish and can be purchased via www.NetworkingGestionandoRelaciones.com

or

www.jordi.pro/books

This book can nurture your network

Have someone from your network benefit from this book!
For £3 plus p&p you can send them a copy of *Connecting Forward*.
You just need to fill this page, tear it off and send it or fax it to:

Troubador Publishing Ltd, 9 Priory Business Park,
Wistow Road, Kibworth, Leicester. LE8 0RX, UK
Fax: +44 116 2792277

Please, send a copy of *Connecting Forward* to the following person:

Name: ....
Address: ....
....
....
....
Postcode: ....
Country: ....

And charge £3 + p&p to my credit/debit card (all major cards accepted, except American Express). *The p&p fees vary according to country of destination. UK £3; Europe £4.50; ROW £8. See www.troubador.co.uk).*

My card details are:
Name on Card: ....
Card Number: ____ ____ ____ ____
Expiry Date: ___ / ____   Start date: ___ / ____
Issue no (Maestro only): ____
CVC number (the last three digits on the back of the card): ___

Signature: